GLOBALVIEWPOINTS

Medical Ethics

Other Books of Related Interest:

At Issue Series
The Right to Die

Current Controversies Series
Human Genetics
Medical Ethics

Global Viewpoints Series
Death and Dying

Introducing Issues with Opposing Viewpoints Series
Death and Dying

GLOBALVIEWPOINTS

Medical Ethics

Diane Andrews Henningfeld, Book Editor

GREENHAVEN PRESS
A part of Gale, Cengage Learning

GALE
CENGAGE Learning·

Detroit • New York • San Francisco • New Haven, Conn • Waterville, Maine • London

Christine Nasso, *Publisher*
Elizabeth Des Chenes, *Managing Editor*

© 2011 Greenhaven Press, a part of Gale, Cengage Learning

Gale and Greenhaven Press are registered trademarks used herein under license.

For more information, contact:
Greenhaven Press
27500 Drake Rd.
Farmington Hills, MI 48331-3535
Or you can visit our Internet site at gale.cengage.com

For product information and technology assistance, contact us at

Gale Customer Support, 1-800-877-4253
For permission to use material from this text or product, submit all requests online at www.cengage.com/permissions

Further permissions questions can be emailed to permissionrequest@cengage.com

Articles in Greenhaven Press anthologies are often edited for length to meet page requirements. In addition, original titles of these works are changed to clearly present the main thesis and to explicitly indicate the author's opinion. Every effort is made to ensure that Greenhaven Press accurately reflects the original intent of the authors. Every effort has been made to trace the owners of copyrighted material.

Cover image © Caro/Alamy.

LIBRARY OF CONGRESS CATALOGING-IN-PUBLICATION DATA

Medical ethics / Diane Andrews Henningfeld, book editor.
    p. cm. -- (Global viewpoints)
    Includes bibliographical references and index.
    ISBN 978-0-7377-5195-6 (hardcover) -- ISBN 978-0-7377-5196-3 (pbk.)
    1. Medical ethics--Juvenile literature. 2. Physicians--Professional ethics. I. Henningfeld, Diane Andrews.
    R724.M29263 2011
    174.2--dc22

                                                            2010042270

Printed in Mexico
2 3 4 5 6 7 15 14 13 12

12/12

Table of Contents:

Foreword   11

Introduction   14

Chapter 1: Establishing Medical Ethics

1. The United Nations Adheres to a Declaration   20
   of Bioethics and Human Rights
   UNESCO
   The members of the United Nations subscribe to a common code of medical and bioethical standards that includes respect for human dignity, protection of life, respect for scientific research, and the promotion of
   equitable access to medical developments.

2. Medical Professionals Around the World   33
   Face Complicated Ethical Codes
   Robert M. Veatch
   Health care professionals find themselves confronted with
   often conflicting ethical codes including the Hippocratic
   Oath, the American Medical Association's Principles of
   Medical Ethics, the World Medical Association's Declara-
   tion of Geneva, and their own religious and moral codes.

3. **European** Medical Professionals Are Guided   41
   by Ethical Principles
   Alzheimer Europe
   In Europe, medical ethics and bioethics are guided by
   several basic principles including respect for patient autonomy; beneficence (acting in the best interest of the
   patient); non-maleficence (avoiding harm to the patient);
   and justice.

4. The **Vatican** Outlines Biomedical Ethics   51
   Julia Duin
   The Vatican rules that cloning, embryonic stem cell research, abortion, and other contemporary medical procedures are not ethical.

5. In **Australia**, Medical Ethics Demand   **58**
Acceptance of Cultural Diversity
David L. Bennett, Peter Chown, and Melissa S.-L. Kang
Because Australia is one of the most multicultural countries in the world, physicians must practice "cultural competence" when treating adolescents from various cultural backgrounds.

6. In **India**, Some Medical Professionals   **67**
Are Not Ethical
Vijay Mahajan
Although doctors exercising criminality remain in the minority in India, the medical profession is experiencing increasing corruption; doctors, the government, and the public must demand ethical behavior from medical professionals.

Periodical and Internet Sources Bibliography   **77**

Chapter 2: Medical Ethics and the End of Life

1. In **India**, Palliative Care Follows   **79**
Ethical Guidelines
Bidhu K. Mohanti
Palliative care physicians and nurses follow mandated ethical guidelines to prevent suffering and to treat patients justly in end-of-life care.

2. In **Ireland**, Ethical Debate on Euthanasia   **90**
Is Banned
Len Doyal
Although doctors withdraw life-sustaining treatment from patients in Ireland, voluntary euthanasia is illegal and cannot be debated.

3. **Australians** Debate the Medical Ethics   **96**
of Euthanasia
Wendy Zukerman
Euthanasia is illegal in Australia and is the topic of ongoing debate in national and regional governmental bodies.

4. In the **United Kingdom**, Euthanasia   103
   Should Be Legal
   Raymond Tallis
   Suffering caused by prolonged medical care and respect
   for a patient's autonomy in choosing to die are two rea-
   sons why euthanasia should be legalized.

5. In the **United Kingdom**, Euthanasia   109
   Should Be Illegal
   Melanie Phillips
   The suggestion that the elderly and demented should be
   able to choose euthanasia is regarded by some citizens of
   the United Kingdom as barbaric and immoral.

6. **Canadian** Ethicists Debate the Definition   116
   of Death
   Stuart Laidlaw
   Deciding when somebody is dead is one of the top medical ethical issues in Canada, because technology allows
   patients to continue living when in the past they would
   have been considered dead.

Periodical and Internet Sources Bibliography   121

Chapter 3: Medical Ethics and Organ Transplantation

1. Worldwide, Doctors Consider Global Organ   123
   Trafficking Unethical
   Debra A. Budiani-Saberi and Francis L. Delmonico
   The growing trend for patients to travel abroad to purchase organs and undergo transplantation forces doctors
   in the patient's home country to confront the ethical implications of organ trafficking.

2. In **Scotland**, a System of Presumed Consent   135
   Would Solve the Organ Shortage
   Anne Johnstone
   Presumed consent, a system by which consent to donate
   organs is presumed unless a person has specifically opted
   out in his lifetime, would increase the number of organs
   available for transplant.

3. **China** Takes Steps Against Organ Trafficking   **142**
Debarati Mukherjee

In China, where most organs for transplants are harvested from executed prisoners or from the illegal transplant tourism trade, the government is instituting a voluntary organ donation program.

4. In **Hong Kong**, Volunteer Organ Donations   **147**
Cause Ethical Dilemmas
Ella Lee

A growing number of people are offering to donate organs to complete strangers in Hong Kong, causing changes in health care policies and a reconsideration of the medical ethics of transplantation.

5. The **European Union** Opposes the Sale   **155**
of Human Organs
Arthur Caplan et al.

After an extensive study of organ transplantation, the Council of Europe definitively outlaws the sale of human bodies or body parts for financial gain and further prohibits organ and tissue trafficking.

Periodical and Internet Sources Bibliography   **163**

Chapter 4: Ethics and Medical Research

1. The World Medical Association Establishes   **165**
Ethical Principles for Medical Research
The World Medical Association

The World Medical Association statement of ethical principles for medical research asserts that while research involving human beings is necessary to improve the diagnosis and treatment of disease, the well-being of the human subjects is the most important ethical consideration.

2. **India** Is a Prime Destination for Unethical   **175**
Clinical Trials
Keya Acharya

The medical community is concerned that medical research is not being adequately regulated or monitored in India, leading to unethical clinical trials involving Indian citizens.

3. In the Southern Hemisphere, Some AIDS   181
   Researchers Use Unethical Practices
   Behzad Hassani
   Because researchers from developed countries have difficulty recruiting patients for clinical trials, they often look to Southern Hemisphere developing countries for subjects, sometimes following unethical research procedures in the process.

4. The **Japanese** Government Tightens Ethical   192
   Guidelines for Medical Research
   Koji Masuda
   Because medical institutions persistently violate ethical guidelines in medical research, the Japanese government has instituted new guidelines and stiffer penalties for violation.

5. In the **United States**, Ethicists Debate Using   198
   Prison Inmates for Medical Testing
   Timothy J. Wiegand
   Although the Institute of Medicine of the National Academy of Sciences has recommended wider use of prison inmates for medical studies, some ethicists point out potential problems with this procedure.

6. In **Singapore**, Ethicists Rule in Favor of   206
   Donating Human Eggs for Research Purposes
   Lim Pin et al.
   The Bioethics Advisory Committee of Singapore cites respect for individuals, reciprocity, proportionality, justice, and sustainability as the ethical principles on which it based its recommendations for the donation of human eggs for research.

Periodical and Internet Sources Bibliography   216
For Further Discussion   217
Organizations to Contact   219
Bibliography of Books   225
Index   228

Foreword

> "The problems of all of humanity can
> only be solved by all of humanity."
> —Swiss author Friedrich Dürrenmatt

Global interdependence has become an undeniable reality. Mass media and technology have increased worldwide access to information and created a society of global citizens. Understanding and navigating this global community is a challenge, requiring a high degree of information literacy and a new level of learning sophistication.

Building on the success of its flagship series, *Opposing Viewpoints*, Greenhaven Press has created the *Global Viewpoints* series to examine a broad range of current, often controversial topics of worldwide importance from a variety of international perspectives. Providing students and other readers with the information they need to explore global connections and think critically about worldwide implications, each *Global Viewpoints* volume offers a panoramic view of a topic of widespread significance.

Drugs, famine, immigration—a broad, international treatment is essential to do justice to social, environmental, health, and political issues such as these. Junior high, high school, and early college students, as well as general readers, can all use *Global Viewpoints* anthologies to discern the complexities relating to each issue. Readers will be able to examine unique national perspectives while, at the same time, appreciating the interconnectedness that global priorities bring to all nations and cultures.

Material in each volume is selected from a diverse range of sources, including journals, magazines, newspapers, nonfiction books, speeches, government documents, pamphlets, organization newsletters, and position papers. *Global Viewpoints* is truly global, with material drawn primarily from international sources available in English and secondarily from U.S. sources with extensive international coverage.

Features of each volume in the *Global Viewpoints* series include:

- An **annotated table of contents** that provides a brief summary of each essay in the volume, including the name of the country or area covered in the essay.

- An **introduction** specific to the volume topic.

- A **world map** to help readers locate the countries or areas covered in the essays.

- For each viewpoint, an **introduction** that contains notes about the author and source of the viewpoint explains why material from the specific country is being presented, summarizes the main points of the viewpoint, and offers three **guided reading questions** to aid in understanding and comprehension.

- **For further discussion** questions that promote critical thinking by asking the reader to compare and contrast aspects of the viewpoints or draw conclusions about perspectives and arguments.

- A worldwide list of **organizations to contact** for readers seeking additional information.

- A **periodical bibliography** for each chapter and a **bibliography of books** on the volume topic to aid in further research.

- A comprehensive **subject index** to offer access to people, places, events, and subjects cited in the text, with the countries covered in the viewpoints highlighted.

Global Viewpoints is designed for a broad spectrum of readers who want to learn more about current events, history, political science, government, international relations, economics, environmental science, world cultures, and sociology— students doing research for class assignments or debates, teachers and faculty seeking to supplement course materials, and others wanting to understand current issues better. By presenting how people in various countries perceive the root causes, current consequences, and proposed solutions to worldwide challenges, *Global Viewpoints* volumes offer readers opportunities to enhance their global awareness and their knowledge of cultures worldwide.

Introduction

"War brings military and medical values into conflict, often overwhelming other moral obligations, such as a doctor's obligation to relieve suffering in the face of military necessity. . . . The physician may rightly be strongly opposed to physical abuse and ill-treatment of detainees in times of war."

—Fred Rosner,
"Ethical Dilemmas for Physicians
in Time of War," March 2010

Primum non nocere is a Latin phrase meaning, "First, do no harm." This statement is one of the most important pillars of medical ethics and is well known to doctors around the world. Medical students learn early in their studies that not harming a patient ought to be the first consideration in any ethical decisions they must make. While autonomy (allowing a patient to choose his or her own course of treatment or refuse treatment altogether), beneficence (doing good for a patient), and justice (providing equal access to treatment and treating patients fairly) are other critical ethical pillars, none has quite the weight that non-maleficence, or not doing harm, carries.

Doctors who serve as physicians in the military or in prisons are often placed in ethically difficult situations. Their medical decision making must take into account the pillars of medical ethics; yet they sometimes are required to take actions that are antithetical to non-maleficence. For example, in some American states, and in some countries around the world, the death penalty is legal. Often, prison doctors are called upon to declare death after the punishment is meted out, or in other circumstances, to actually administer lethal doses of drugs. In the first case, being present at an execution and acting in an official capacity to declare that a prisoner is dead as the result of the execution places the doctor in a position of being complicit with the execution. His or her action can thus be interpreted as doing harm.

The American Medical Association's (AMA's) code of ethics is very clear on doctor participation in the implementation of the death penalty: "A physician, as a member of a profession dedicated to preserving life when there is hope of doing so, should not be a participant in a legally authorized execution." Further, the AMA defines participation as anything ranging from prescribing or administering tranquilizers to monitoring prisoner vital signs; being present at an execution; giving technical advice; or actually starting an intravenous line for a lethal injection.

Nonetheless, while the AMA's stance is clear, the organization has never sanctioned a doctor for such participation. Neither has any state medical board ever punished a physician for helping the state execute a prisoner. In North Carolina, the state medical board attempted to ban doctor participation in executions in 2007; however, the state supreme court ruled against the ban in May 2009. Thus, North Carolina joined states such as Florida and California that require a doctor to be present and to participate in executions. The ethical dilemma for doctors, then, is one of serving their states or of serving the medical ethical code of doing no harm.

Doctors living in countries under dictatorships can be faced with even more troubling ethical decisions concerning non-maleficence. In modern times, the most egregious example of doctors ignoring the ethical precept of non-maleficence took place in Nazi Germany and Nazi-controlled countries between 1933 and 1945. Doctors performed unspeakable acts of torture and violence against Jews and other prisoners, all in the name of medical science.

In 1946, after the close of World War II, the United States, Britain, the Soviet Union, and France collectively held a tribunal in Nuremberg, Germany, to try Nazi military personnel and doctors on charges of crimes against humanity. The doctors attempted to defend themselves by stating that they were conducting "necessary wartime research" and that they were "following the orders of their superiors," according to George J. Annas, writing in the *New England Journal of Medicine* in May 2005. At the conclusion of the trials, the members of the tribunal drafted the Nuremberg Principles, stating in part "there are crimes against humanity (such as torture), that individuals can be held to be criminally responsible for committing them, and that obeying orders is no defense." The Nuremberg Principles thus hold doctors responsible for not violating the ethical pillar of non-maleficence.

There is also evidence that doctors participated in torture and even murder during the regime of Chilean president Augusto Pinochet Ugarte, who ruled from 1973 to 1990. During this period, according to Scott Horton, writing in the December 18, 2009, issue of *Harper's*, former Chilean president Eduardo Frei Montalva was killed by "a conspiracy of doctors" who injected the president with lethal doses of toxins while he was undergoing routine medical procedures. In addition, many people in Chile were tortured or killed, often with the compliance and help of medical personnel. For example, Benjamin Vergara describes his experience of torture in the September 11, 2003, issue of the *Guardian*. After being arrested, tortured, and released, he was again detained and tortured, this time with doctors in the room. During the torture, he states, "three times I stopped breathing and my heart stopped. One of the doctors present in the torture chamber resuscitated me." While the doctor was acting ethically in that he saved his patient's life, he nonetheless violated the precept of non-maleficence, in that his intervention allowed Vergara's captors to engage in more torture.

Medical ethics and harming patients continues to be an important consideration in the twenty-first century. As Annas argues, "The question of torture during wartime, and the role of physicians in torture, is again a source of consternation and controversy." The detention center at Guantánamo Bay where prisoners from the war on terror have been held since 2002 and the prison at Abu Ghraib, Iraq, illustrate the heart of the controversy.

Former secretary of defense Donald Rumsfeld's policy for the interrogation of prisoners called for the inclusion of medical personnel in the procedure, according to a memo from Rumsfeld to the commander of the U.S. Southern Command, dated April 16, 2003. Medical personnel not only provided routine care for prisoners, but they were also required to certify that the prisoners were healthy enough, both mentally and physically, to withstand intense interrogative techniques such as waterboarding. In addition, they provided care for prisoners after interrogation, helping to make the prisoners fit for more sessions. Part of the controversy derives from differing definitions for the word "torture;" however, there is ample evidence that some prisoners in the war on terror were harmed, either emotionally or physically, by interrogation techniques.

Those who defend the actions of the interrogators and the medical personnel participating at Guantánamo and Abu Ghraib argue that the war on terror is a new kind of combat demanding a new kind of ethics. However, many doctors and ethicists believe that such participation by medical personnel is not ethical and violates the precept of non-maleficence.

The role of medical staff in prisons is only one concern of medical ethics, however. The viewpoints that follow consider how medical ethics are established; the role of ethics in end-of-life care; the ethics of organ transplantation; and issues of ethical medical research.

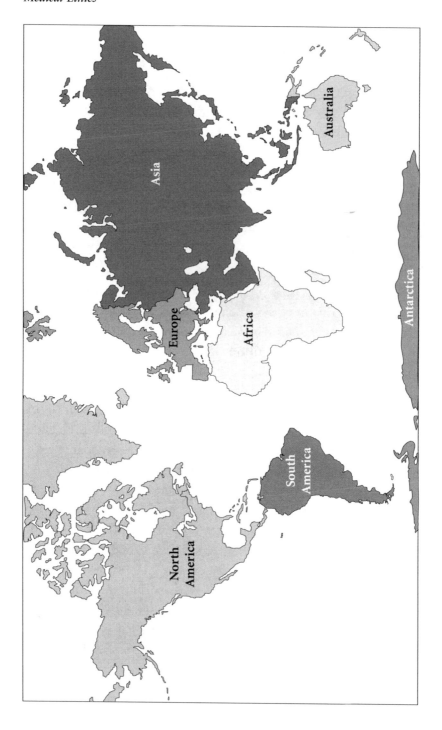

CHAPTER 1

Establishing Medical Ethics

The United Nations Adheres to a Declaration of Bioethics and Human Rights

UNESCO

In the following viewpoint, the United Nations Educational, Scientific and Cultural Organization (UNESCO) issues a statement of ethical medical principles that all member nations are encouraged to abide by. This "Universal Declaration on Bioethics and Human Rights" is intended to promote the ethical treatment of all human beings while still allowing freedom for medical research. It also includes statements regarding equal access to medical developments and provides guidance for the implementation of the principles. UNESCO is a specialized agency of the United Nations with a purpose to encourage peace by promoting collaboration among all nations in areas of education, science, and culture.

As you read, consider the following questions:

1. To whom is the declaration addressed?
2. According to the declaration, scientific research should only be carried out with what?
3. What should be the role of independent, multidisciplinary, and pluralist ethics committees, under the provisions of the doctrine?

"Universal Declaration on Bioethics and Human Rights," United Nations Educational, Scientific and Cultural Organization (UNESCO), October 19, 2005. Reproduced by permission.

GENERAL PROVISIONS

Article 1 — Scope

1. This Declaration addresses ethical issues related to medicine, life sciences and associated technologies as applied to human beings, taking into account their social, legal and environmental dimensions.

2. This Declaration is addressed to [United Nations Member] States. As appropriate and relevant, it also provides guidance to decisions or practices of individuals, groups, communities, institutions and corporations, public and private.

Article 2 — Aims

The aims of this Declaration are:

(a) to provide a universal framework of principles and procedures to guide States in the formulation of their legislation, policies or other instruments in the field of bioethics;

(b) to guide the actions of individuals, groups, communities, institutions and corporations, public and private;

(c) to promote respect for human dignity and protect human rights, by ensuring respect for the life of human beings, and fundamental freedoms, consistent with international human rights law;

(d) to recognize the importance of freedom of scientific research and the benefits derived from scientific and technological developments, while stressing the need for such research and developments to occur within the framework of ethical principles set out in this Declaration and to respect human dignity, human rights and fundamental freedoms;

(e) to foster multidisciplinary and pluralistic dialogue about bioethical issues between all stakeholders and within society as a whole;

(f) to promote equitable access to medical, scientific and technological developments as well as the greatest possible flow and the rapid sharing of knowledge concerning those developments and the sharing of benefits, with particular attention to the needs of developing countries;

(g) to safeguard and promote the interests of the present and future generations;

(h) to underline the importance of biodiversity and its conservation as a common concern of humankind.

PRINCIPLES OF THE DECLARATION

Within the scope of this Declaration, in decisions or practices taken or carried out by those to whom it is addressed, the following principles are to be respected.

Article 3—Human Dignity and Human Rights

1. Human dignity, human rights and fundamental freedoms are to be fully respected.

2. The interests and welfare of the individual should have priority over the sole interest of science or society.

The interests and welfare of the individual should have priority over the sole interest of science or society.

Article 4—Benefit and Harm

In applying and advancing scientific knowledge, medical practice and associated technologies, direct and indirect benefits to patients, research participants and other affected individuals should be maximized and any possible harm to such individuals should be minimized.

Article 5—Autonomy and Individual Responsibility

The autonomy of persons to make decisions, while taking responsibility for those decisions and respecting the autonomy of others, is to be respected. For persons who are not capable of exercising autonomy, special measures are to be taken to protect their rights and interests.

Article 6—Consent

1. Any preventive, diagnostic and therapeutic medical intervention is only to be carried out with the prior, free and informed consent of the person concerned, based on adequate information. The consent should, where appropriate, be expressed and may be withdrawn by the person concerned at any time and for any reason without disadvantage or prejudice.

2. Scientific research should only be carried out with the prior, free, express and informed consent of the person concerned. The information should be adequate, provided in a comprehensible form and should include modalities for withdrawal of consent. Consent may be withdrawn by the person concerned at any time and for any reason without any disadvantage or prejudice. Exceptions to this principle should be made only in accordance with ethical and legal standards adopted by States, consistent with the principles and provisions set out in this Declaration, in particular in Article 27, and international human rights law.

3. In appropriate cases of research carried out on a group of persons or a community, additional agreement of the legal representatives of the group or community concerned may be sought. In no case should a collective community agreement or the consent of a community leader or other authority substitute for an individual's informed consent.

Article 7—Persons Without the Capacity to Consent

In accordance with domestic law, special protection is to be given to persons who do not have the capacity to consent:

(a) authorization for research and medical practice should be obtained in accordance with the best interest of the person concerned and in accordance with domestic law. However, the person concerned should be involved to the greatest extent possible in the decision-making process of consent, as well as that of withdrawing consent;

(b) research should only be carried out for his or her direct health benefit, subject to the authorization and the protective conditions prescribed by law, and if there is no research alternative of comparable effectiveness with research participants able to consent. Research which does not have potential direct health benefit should only be undertaken by way of exception, with the utmost restraint, exposing the person only to a minimal risk and minimal burden and, if the research is expected to contribute to the health benefit of other persons in the same category, subject to the conditions prescribed by law and compatible with the protection of the individual's human rights. Refusal of such persons to take part in research should be respected.

Article 8—Respect for Human Vulnerability and Personal Integrity

In applying and advancing scientific knowledge, medical practice and associated technologies, human vulnerability should be taken into account. Individuals and groups of special vulnerability should be protected and the personal integrity of such individuals respected.

Article 9—Privacy and Confidentiality

The privacy of the persons concerned and the confidentiality of their personal information should be respected. To the greatest extent possible, such information should not be used or disclosed for purposes other than those for which it was collected or consented to, consistent with international law, in particular international human rights law.

The fundamental equality of all human beings in dignity and rights is to be respected so that they are treated justly and equitably.

Article 10—Equality, Justice and Equity

The fundamental equality of all human beings in dignity and rights is to be respected so that they are treated justly and equitably.

Article 11—Non-Discrimination and Non-Stigmatization

No individual or group should be discriminated against or stigmatized on any grounds, in violation of human dignity, human rights and fundamental freedoms.

Article 12—Respect for Cultural Diversity and Pluralism

The importance of cultural diversity and pluralism should be given due regard. However, such considerations are not to be invoked to infringe upon human dignity, human rights and fundamental freedoms, nor upon the principles set out in this Declaration, nor to limit their scope.

Article 13—Solidarity and Cooperation

Solidarity among human beings and international cooperation towards that end are to be encouraged.

Article 14—Social Responsibility and Health

1. The promotion of health and social development for their people is a central purpose of governments that all sectors of society share.

2. Taking into account that the enjoyment of the highest attainable standard of health is one of the fundamental rights of every human being without distinction of race, religion, political belief, economic or social condition, progress in science and technology should advance:

    (a) access to quality health care and essential medicines, especially for the health of women and children, because health is essential to life itself and must be considered to be a social and human good;

    (b) access to adequate nutrition and water;

    (c) improvement of living conditions and the environment;

    (d) elimination of the marginalization and the exclusion of persons on the basis of any grounds;

    (e) reduction of poverty and illiteracy.

Article 15—Sharing of Benefits

1. Benefits resulting from any scientific research and its applications should be shared with society as a whole and within the international community, in particular with developing countries. In giving effect to this principle, benefits may take any of the following forms:

    (a) special and sustainable assistance to, and acknowledgement of, the persons and groups that have taken part in the research;

    (b) access to quality health care;

    (c) provision of new diagnostic and therapeutic modalities or products stemming from research;

    (d) support for health services;

(e) access to scientific and technological knowledge;

(f) capacity-building facilities for research purposes;

(g) other forms of benefit consistent with the principles set out in this Declaration.

2. Benefits should not constitute improper inducements to participate in research.

The impact of life sciences on future generations, including on their genetic constitution, should be given due regard.

Article 16—Protecting Future Generations

The impact of life sciences on future generations, including on their genetic constitution, should be given due regard.

Article 17—Protection of the Environment, the Biosphere and Biodiversity

Due regard is to be given to the interconnection between human beings and other forms of life, to the importance of appropriate access and utilization of biological and genetic resources, to respect for traditional knowledge and to the role of human beings in the protection of the environment, the biosphere and biodiversity.

APPLICATION OF THE PRINCIPLES

Article 18—Decision-Making and Addressing Bioethical Issues

1. Professionalism, honesty, integrity and transparency in decision-making should be promoted, in particular declarations of all conflicts of interest and appropriate sharing of knowledge. Every endeavour should be made to use the best available scientific knowledge and methodology in addressing and periodically reviewing bioethical issues.

Human Rights and Medical Ethics

The professional regulatory system known as medical ethics has been one of the most visionary and socially valuable creations of the medical profession. Its beneficial influence has extended beyond physician/patient relations, to the shaping of many key humanistic and egalitarian features of the world's legal and political institutions. The continued existence of medical ethics as a professionally influential normative system, however, is being challenged by international human rights. The UNESCO [United Nations Educational, Scientific and Cultural Organization] "Universal Declaration on Bioethics and Human Rights," I will argue, is likely to be an important point of intersection in this process.

Medical ethics has played morally inspirational, educational, disciplinary, and normative roles from its location in traditional professional oaths, codes prepared by medical associations, as well as guidelines applied by clinical and research ethics committees. Contemporary medical ethics is conceptually enriched by influential texts and academic articles summarising and categorising its core professional virtues and principles.

T.A. Faunce,
"Will International Human Rights Subsume Medical Ethics?
Intersections in the UNESCO Universal Bioethics Declaration,"
Journal of Medical Ethics, *vol. 31, no. 3, March 2005.*

2. Persons and professionals concerned and society as a whole should be engaged in dialogue on a regular basis.

3. Opportunities for informed pluralistic public debate, seeking the expression of all relevant opinions, should be promoted.

Article 19—Ethics Committees

Independent, multidisciplinary and pluralist ethics committees should be established, promoted and supported at the appropriate level in order to:

(a) assess the relevant ethical, legal, scientific and social issues related to research projects involving human beings;

(b) provide advice on ethical problems in clinical settings;

(c) assess scientific and technological developments, formulate recommendations and contribute to the preparation of guidelines on issues within the scope of this Declaration;

(d) foster debate, education and public awareness of, and engagement in, bioethics.

Article 20—Risk Assessment and Management

Appropriate assessment and adequate management of risk related to medicine, life sciences and associated technologies should be promoted.

Article 21—Transnational Practices

1. States, public and private institutions, and professionals associated with transnational activities should endeavour to ensure that any activity within the scope of this Declaration, undertaken, funded or otherwise pursued in whole or in part in different States, is consistent with the principles set out in this Declaration.

2. When research is undertaken or otherwise pursued in one or more States (the host State(s)) and funded by a source in another State, such research should be the object of an appropriate level of ethical review in the host State(s) and the State in which the funder is located. This review should be based on ethical and legal standards that are consistent with the principles set out in this Declaration.

3. Transnational health research should be responsive to the needs of host countries, and the importance of research contributing to the alleviation of urgent global health problems should be recognized.

4. When negotiating a research agreement, terms for collaboration and agreement on the benefits of research should be established with equal participation by those party to the negotiation.

5. States should take appropriate measures, both at the national and international levels, to combat bioterrorism and illicit traffic in organs, tissues, samples, genetic resources and genetic-related materials.

PROMOTION OF THE DECLARATION

Article 22—Role of States

1. States should take all appropriate measures, whether of a legislative, administrative or other character, to give effect to the principles set out in this Declaration in accordance with international human rights law. Such measures should be supported by action in the spheres of education, training and public information.

2. States should encourage the establishment of independent, multidisciplinary and pluralist ethics committees, as set out in Article 19.

Article 23—Bioethics Education, Training and Information

1. In order to promote the principles set out in this Declaration and to achieve a better understanding of the ethical implications of scientific and technological developments, in particular for young people, States should endeavour to foster bioethics education and training at all levels as well as to encourage information and knowledge dissemination programmes about bioethics.

2. States should encourage the participation of international and regional intergovernmental organizations and international, regional and national nongovernmental organizations in this endeavour.

Article 24—International Cooperation

1. States should foster international dissemination of scientific information and encourage the free flow and sharing of scientific and technological knowledge.

2. Within the framework of international cooperation, States should promote cultural and scientific cooperation and enter into bilateral and multilateral agreements enabling developing countries to build up their capacity to participate in generating and sharing scientific knowledge, the related know-how and the benefits thereof.

3. States should respect and promote solidarity between and among States, as well as individuals, families, groups and communities, with special regard for those rendered vulnerable by disease or disability or other personal, societal or environmental conditions and those with the most limited resources.

Article 25—Follow-Up Action by UNESCO

1. UNESCO [United Nations Educational, Scientific and Cultural Organization] shall promote and disseminate the principles set out in this Declaration. In doing so, UNESCO should seek the help and assistance of the Intergovernmental Bioethics Committee (IGBC) and the International Bioethics Committee (IBC).

2. UNESCO shall reaffirm its commitment to dealing with bioethics and to promoting collaboration between IGBC and IBC.

FINAL PROVISIONS

Article 26—Interrelation and Complementarity of the Principles

This Declaration is to be understood as a whole and the principles are to be understood as complementary and interrelated. Each principle is to be considered in the context of the other principles, as appropriate and relevant in the circumstances.

Article 27—Limitations on the Application of the Principles

If the application of the principles of this Declaration is to be limited, it should be by law, including laws in the interests of public safety, for the investigation, detection and prosecution of criminal offences, for the protection of public health or for the protection of the rights and freedoms of others. Any such law needs to be consistent with international human rights law.

Article 28—Denial of Acts Contrary to Human Rights, Fundamental Freedoms and Human Dignity

Nothing in this Declaration may be interpreted as implying for any State, group or person any claim to engage in any activity or to perform any act contrary to human rights, fundamental freedoms and human dignity.

Medical Professionals Around the World Face Complicated Ethical Codes

Robert M. Veatch

In the following viewpoint, Robert M. Veatch describes the many, often contradictory, ethical codes with which doctors and other health professionals must contend. He urges health professionals to think closely about the source of their own ethical norms and to consider what they must do when their religious or philosophical codes conflict with professional codes. He argues that professionally established codes must yield to the religious and philosophical codes of ethics of both doctors and patients. Veatch is a professor of biomedical ethics at the Kennedy Institute of Ethics at Georgetown University.

As you read, consider the following questions:

1. What is the "grand-daddy" of professional codes for physicians, according to Veatch?
2. What conflict of ethics does the authority say Jewish medical students might encounter at secular schools?
3. According to Veatch, what does Kantian ethics explicitly reject?

Robert M. Veatch, "The Sources of Professional Ethics: Why Professions Fail," *The Lancet*, vol. 373, no. 9668, March 21, 2009, pp. 1000–1001. Copyright © 2009 Elsevier Limited. All rights reserved. Reproduced by permission.

One of the defining characteristics of professions has always been that they have their own codes of ethics and are responsible for professional discipline. While professional ethics used to be thought of as something of a platitude, today all of that is changing. We can quickly see the problem if we ask what the source of professional ethics ought to be.

The classic answer was that it comes from the professional group. Until recently, the profession was assumed to have custody of its ethics code. It had the responsibility to articulate its content and enforce its norms. Even if we assume this is true, however, we are discovering problems. Different professional groups within medicine (or any other profession) write codes and try to enforce them. In medicine, the classic code [of ethics], the Hippocratic Oath, exists alongside many written by national, regional, and international professional bodies. The British Medical Association (BMA) and similar national bodies have codified their understanding of the moral norms, but so have many local and, in the USA, statewide organisations. The World Medical Association (WMA) has written the Declaration of Geneva.

Conflicting Ethical Codes

Here's the hooker: These codes are, at times, significantly different. A physician who is a member of the American Medical Association (AMA) is expected to adhere to its Principles of Medical Ethics, but those principles are sometimes at odds with the WMA's Declaration of Geneva. Moreover, national bodies often claim that their codes apply to members of the profession practising in their jurisdiction even if the individual is not a member of the professional organisation or even not a citizen of the country. In the USA, about half of all physicians are not AMA members, yet we often assume their norms apply to all physicians. Some code provisions are controversial. The AMA and BMA codes before the 1970s permitted confidentiality breaches to benefit patients (even if the patients did not agree). They did not permit breaching confidences to protect others (say, if the patient is threatening to hurt someone or is likely to spread an infectious disease). Since then, codes have changed, making paternalistic disclosures to protect patients morally suspect, but opening the door to non-paternalistic disclosures to protect third parties. Meanwhile, the WMA's Declaration of Geneva simply makes a blank-cheque exceptionless promise of confidentiality. In some jurisdictions, following the Declaration of Geneva violates laws that require reporting or warning that patients may pose potential harm to others.

The grand-daddy of professional codes for physicians, the Hippocratic Oath, is even more controversial. Hippocratic physicians pledge not to reveal their knowledge of medicine to lay people (not here pledging to keep patients' information confidential, but rather promising not to disclose the secret knowledge of remedies or healing theories). The old Greek cultic oath appears to prohibit abortion; it prohibits giving deadly drugs; it even prohibits the practice of surgery. These provisions often conflict with national professional codes. Surely, no morally responsible physician today can pledge without qualification to practise medicine Hippocratically.

Medical Schools Commit Students to a Variety of Codes

In teaching medical ethics to medical students I have asked them which professional code they consider most appropriate for moral guidance. The answers vary widely. All the standard codes are named. This means that, if the students understand what they are saying, they may well be committing to a moral code that differs from that of their fellow students, indeed, a study of North American medical schools in 1993 found different schools committing their students variously to the Hippocratic Oath, the Declaration of Geneva, the Prayer of Maimonides, or various other oaths and codes some of which were written by the individual faculties or student groups. This might not be a problem if one assumed that they all said more or less the same thing—something like pledging to benefit the patient and protect the patient from harm. They don't all say this, however, and even if they did, it is now clear that physicians sometimes have a duty to refrain from benefiting their patients. For example, most now accept the idea that patients have the right to refuse consent to treatment.

The problem is even more complex when one realises that physicians are simultaneously members of other groups. Many, for example, are members of religious organisations. It is the nature of religions that they claim ultimate authority on moral matters. These claims include matters of professional moral behaviour. The Catholic doctor, for example, typically holds views about abortion, euthanasia, and more subtle issues. A Catholic emergency room physician may simultaneously receive moral guidance from her professional group requiring unbiased counselling of rape victims while receiving a moral mandate from her church that excludes certain options as morally intolerable. Jewish medical students at secular schools receive professionally generated moral guidance on forgoing life support that is out of sync with rabbinical teachings. Even physicians who profess no religious affiliation stand in some moral tradition that commands allegiance. They may be utilitarians, feminists, Kantians [those who follow the teachings of Immanuel Kant, an eighteenth-century German philosopher], Marxists [those who follow the teachings of Karl Marx, a nineteenth-century German philosopher], or proponents of secular liberal political philosophy or human rights. These schools of ethical thought each provide certain moral principles that include guidance for practising medicine.

Sometimes these traditions clash with professionally generated codes. The Hippocratic imperative that the physician should focus exclusively on the welfare of the individual patient is incompatible with the utilitarian imperative that our actions should be structured to maximise aggregate net utility. One cannot be Kantian and Hippocratic about truth-telling to patients at the same time.

The horrible reality is that professionally generated moral norms may in very real ways be incompatible with religious and secular philosophical traditions in which physicians see themselves standing.

A Horrible Reality

The horrible reality is that professionally generated moral norms may in very real ways be incompatible with religious and secular philosophical traditions in which physicians see themselves standing. Moreover, these moral traditions outside of the profession often have a more plausible claim to be morally authoritative. Churches have beliefs about how their members have knowledge of the deity. One committed to such a tradition acknowledges what philosophers would call "epistemological authority", that is, knowledge of the divine will. It is a claim that normally professions are not in a position to make. If religiously committed physicians perceive that the profession holds moral norms that are incompatible with religious norms, surely it is the religious authority that is ultimate, not the profession. Many religious teachings—about killing, honesty, fidelity to promises, and respect for human dignity—may clash with the positions held by the professional group. The physician has to choose between the two sources of authority and normally would give the religious teaching the highest status.

The same holds for secular physicians who accept certain moral norms about human rights. If the physician's professional group adopts a position at odds with the norms of the secular philosophical tradition, surely the tradition outside the profession has to win out. For centuries many professional medical ethics permitted physicians to lie to patients about

The Hippocratic Oath

I swear . . . by all the gods . . . making them judges, to bring the following oath and written covenant to fulfillment, in accordance with my power and my judgment;

to regard him who has taught me this techné, [art and science] as equal to my parents . . .

and to give a share both of rules and of lectures, and of all the rest of learning, to my sons and to the [sons] of him who has taught me. . . .

And I will use regimens for the benefit of the ill in accordance with my ability and my judgment, but from [what is] to their harm or injustice I will keep [them].

And I will not give a drug that is deadly to anyone if asked [for it], nor will I suggest the way to such a counsel.

And likewise I will not give a woman a destructive pessary. . . .

I will not cut, and certainly not those suffering from stone, but I will cede [this] to men [who are] practitioners of this activity.

Into as many houses as I may enter, I will go for the benefit of the ill, while being far from all voluntary and destructive injustice, especially from sexual acts both upon women's bodies and upon men's, both of the free and of the slaves.

And about whatever I may see or hear in treatment, or even without treatment, in the life of human beings—things that should not ever be blurted out outside—I will remain silent, holding such things to be unutterable [sacred, not to be divulged]. . . .

Steven H. Miles, "The Oath,"
The Hippocratic Oath and the Ethics of Medicine.
New York: Oxford University Press, 2004, pp. xiii–xiv.

terminal diagnoses to spare patients the suffering that would accompany the bad news. That defence of the benevolent lie is explicitly rejected by Kantian ethics and other moral traditions outside of medicine. Physicians caught between the two who are simultaneously members of the profession and committed Kantians ought reasonably to view Kantianism as more authoritative. There is nothing about a professional group that gives it a claim to be authoritative on the ethics of lying. There is everything about Kantianism that makes such a claim.

Professional sources of norms have to yield to religious and secular sources.

A final problem confronts physicians trying to determine the source of their professional ethics. Suppose physicians can figure out which of the many conflicting professional sources of moral norms for medicine is authoritative. Suppose they can figure out whether religious and secular moral traditions take precedence over professionally articulated norms. Physicians still must work together with patients. Patients also have moral views about the lay-professional relation: views about whether consent refusals should be honoured, about whether it is morally preferable to be sheltered from a terminal diagnosis, and about confidentiality, mercy killing, and countless other morally sensitive issues. The moral norms that govern the lay-professional relation are not the exclusive province of the professional. One of the difficulties with moral codifications generated by professional groups is that one of the two parties in the lay-professional relation is excluded. If ethics comes from the professional group, no layperson has standing to influence that code. From the patient's point of view, the professionally generated codes are foreign. They are like moral norms coming from a private club in which patients cannot be members. Those codes can have no standing, no basis for respect. One alternative to professionally generated codifications is, for example, UNESCO's [United Nations Educational, Scientific and Cultural Organization's] "Universal Declaration on Bioethics and Human Rights", which is an international public document.

Professional Norms Must Yield

The time has come for professionals and laypeople to think more about which sources of norms command loyalty. Health professionals face a dilemma. Many different professional groups articulate codes vying for physician loyalty. Those professionally generated codes contain major differences so, at minimum, professionals must decide which should claim their adherence. More critically, physicians who are committed to some religious or secular worldview have to decide which tradition is morally authoritative. Normally, those committed to a religious or secular philosophical tradition would find these moral norms outside the profession take precedence over professional norms. Most critically, physicians have to understand that patients also bring moral views to the relation that the patient considers authoritative. Ideally, a moral meeting of the minds will occur so that layperson and professional can share common moral worldviews. These shared norms may be incompatible with morality coming from professional sources. Since patients are not part of the professional tradition, that source will have to be from outside of medicine. Professional sources of norms have to yield to religious and secular sources.

European Medical Professionals Are Guided by Ethical Principles

Alzheimer Europe

In the following viewpoint, Alzheimer Europe contends that bio-ethics in Europe is based on solidarity, freedom, tolerance, equal opportunity, social justice, and human dignity. Alzheimer Europe stresses the importance of autonomy of the patient in decision making. It also notes the importance of physicians doing good work and not causing harm. In addition, ensuring that all patients are treated equally is another important European ethical standard. Alzheimer Europe is a nonprofit organization aimed at improving care and treatment of patients with Alzheimer's disease.

As you read, consider the following questions:

1. What does Kant's Categorical Imperative state?
2. What does the concept of autonomy involve for nineteenth-century British philosopher John Stuart Mill?
3. What is the principle of beneficence and non-maleficence, according to the author?

The term "medical ethics" is often used to refer to the deontology [the study of the nature of duty and obligation] of the medical profession covering issues such as moral rules,

Alzheimer Europe, "Medical Ethics and Bioethics in Europe," and "The Four Common Bioethical Principles," Alzheimer Europe, October 9, 2009 and March 29, 2010. Reproduced by permission.

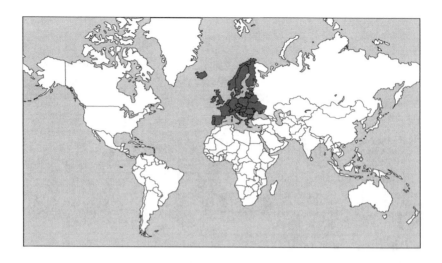

rules of etiquette and rules for professional conduct. The word "deontological" comes from the root "deon" which means duty or obligation in Latin. In some countries, codes or medical ethics have been supplemented by patients' rights laws. There is a difference between the two in that the former emphasizes the obligations and duties of doctors whereas the latter usually involves some form of legal right or entitlement. Nevertheless, in some countries codes of medical ethics are enshrined in law and consequently take on a legal status (with regard to the obligations of health care professionals). [David Couzens] Hoy argues that obligations which are enforced and hence not undertaken freely, are not in the realm of the ethical. For example, in countries where slavery has been abolished or certain forms of animal experimentation made illegal, such issues move from the realm of the ethical to that of the legal. On the other hand, certain practices such as abortion or euthanasia have been legalized in some countries but are not accepted [by] some groups in society as being ethical.

Bioethics Defined

The term "bioethics" was used for the first time by [Van Rensselaer] Potter, a biologist, in 1970 to refer to ethical problems linked to the present and the future of life in general and of human life in particular. Later, [André] Hellegers used the term to refer to a way to approach and resolve the moral conflicts raised by modern medicine.

In Europe, bioethics is very much based on the principle of solidarity, as well as freedom, tolerance, equal opportunity, social justice and human dignity.

Bioethics is not just a series of principles but implies, in the European tradition at least, a moral obligation to act. [Immanuel] Kant, a German philosopher from the Enlightenment period [eighteenth century], was concerned with the motivation behind any action. He stated that action done from duty has its moral worth not in the purpose to be attained by it but in the maxim in accordance with which it is decided upon. He developed the Categorical Imperative which states, "Act only on that maxim whereby you can at the same time will that it should become a universal law or a universal law of nature."

In Europe, bioethics is very much based on the principle of solidarity, as well as freedom, tolerance, equal opportunity, social justice and human dignity. The gradual and continued expansion of the European Union [EU] had led to new possibilities and potential problems in the health care domain. At the same time, efforts are constantly under way to harmonise health care provision, promote cooperation and find consensus on a variety of health care issues. In 1992, the Maastricht Treaty [Treaty on European Union] made public health an object of EU policy.

However, long before this, the Council of Europe had decided to set up a single specialised committee to deal with bioethical issues. This committee, the Steering Committee on Bioethics, was granted permanent status in 1992. This came just one year after the Commission of the European Union set up the Group of Advisers on the Ethical Implications of Biotechnology (GAEIB).

In 1997, the Council of Europe's Convention on Human Rights and Biomedicine was signed by 21 member states in Oviedo, Spain. Its emphasis on the principles of human dignity and solidarity can be clearly detected in some of the recitals of the preamble:

- Convinced of the need to respect the human being both as an individual and as a member of the human species and recognising the importance of ensuring the dignity of the human being;

- Conscious that the misuse of biology and medicine may lead to acts endangering human dignity;

- Affirming that progress in biology and medicine should be used for the benefit of present and future generations;

- Stressing the need for international co-operation so that all humanity may enjoy the benefits of biology and medicine;

- Wishing to remind all members of society of their rights and responsibilities.

The Four Common Bioethical Principles

The word *autonomy* comes from the Greek *autos-nomos* meaning "self-rule" or "self-determination". According to Kantian ethics, autonomy is based on the human capacity to direct one's life according to rational principles. . . .

Rationality, in Kant's view, is the means to autonomy. Autonomous people are considered as being ends in themselves in that they have the capacity to determine their own destiny, and as such must be respected.

For John Stuart Mill [a nineteenth-century British philosopher] the concept of respect for autonomy involves the capacity to think, decide and act on the basis of such thought and decision freely and independently. Mill advocated the principle of autonomy (or the principle of liberty as he called it) provided that it did not cause harm to others. . . .

The Principle of Autonomy

The principle of not causing harm to others (known as Mill's "harm principle") provides the grounds for the moral right of a patient to refuse medical treatment and for a doctor to refrain from intervening against the patient's wishes. Nevertheless, Mill believed that it was acceptable to prevent people from harming themselves provided that their action was not fully informed.

Nowadays, an autonomous decision might be described as one that is made freely/without undue influence, by a competent person, in full knowledge and understanding of the relevant information necessary to make such a decision. It should also be applicable to the current situation or circumstances.

Self-determination is a central principle in health care, which is gradually moving away from a paternalistic approach towards a more individualistic, client-centred approach where the patient plays a more active role.

Many people see dementia as a humiliating disease involving a deterioration of mental power, the loss of one's former personality and identity and eventually becoming a burden to others. Many dread the prospect of being deprived of the chance to decide their own fate and thus exercise their right to self-determination. Fears linked to this perception of dementia may include the fear of under-treatment (on the grounds that dementia cannot be cured) and the fear of over-treatment, thereby prolonging the suffering that accompanies dementia.

Self-determination is a central principle in health care, which is gradually moving away from a paternalistic approach towards a more individualistic, client-centred approach where the patient plays a more active role in his/her own health and well-being. Such an approach requires that patients take responsibility for making their own decisions and also that they bear the consequences of those choices.

However, it should be borne in mind that not everyone agrees with the emphasis that is currently placed on autonomy. For example, although the Danish Council of Ethics appreciates individuals taking responsibility for their own lives, it points out that the ideal of personal autonomy is based on extreme individualism and that this viewpoint takes the focus away from the fact that people are always influenced and to some extent dependent on others. They are what they are as a result of interactions with others and a particular history. Similarly, the Finnish National Advisory Board on Health Care Ethics—ETENE—cautions against concentrating almost exclusively on the principles of autonomy and self-determination. . . .

Nevertheless, the possibility to exercise some degree of autonomy, through advance consent or refusal of medical treatment and/or care, could be beneficial to many people with dementia.

The Principles of Beneficence and Non-Maleficence

As the principles of beneficence and non-maleficence are closely related, they are discussed together in this section. Beneficence involves balancing the benefits of treatment against the risks and costs involved, whereas non-maleficence means avoiding the causation of harm. As many treatments involve

European Nations That Have Signed or Ratified the Oviedo Convention on Human Rights and Biomedicine

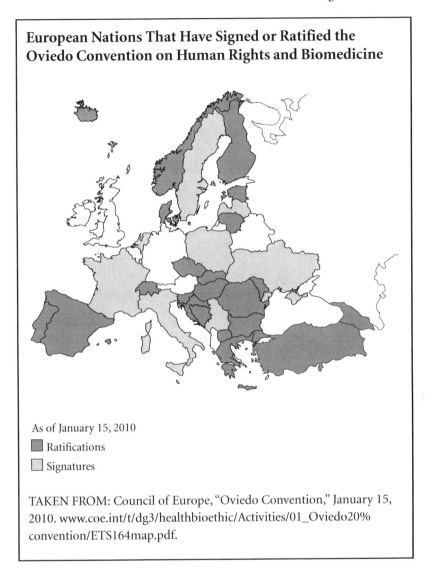

As of January 15, 2010

■ Ratifications

□ Signatures

TAKEN FROM: Council of Europe, "Oviedo Convention," January 15, 2010. www.coe.int/t/dg3/healthbioethic/Activities/01_Oviedo20% convention/ETS164map.pdf.

some degree of harm, the principle of non-maleficence would imply that the harm should not be disproportionate to the benefit of the treatment. Respecting the principles of beneficence and non-maleficence may in certain circumstances mean failing to respect a person's *autonomy*, i.e., respecting their views about a particular treatment. For example, it may be necessary to provide treatment that is not desired in order to prevent the development of a future, more serious health problem. The treatment might be unpleasant, uncomfortable or even painful but this might involve less harm to the patient than would occur, were they not to have it.

In cases where the patient lacks legal competence to make a decision, medical staff is expected to act in the best interests of the patient. In doing so, they may take into account the principles of beneficence and non-maleficence. However, it would be helpful for medical staff in such cases if the patient lacking capacity had made an advance directive. Nevertheless, ... problems may arise when there is a conflict between what a person requested in an advance directive and what in the doctor's view is in their best interests, particularly in cases where it is no longer clear that the person in question would still agree with the decision previously made.

In Western medicine, the principles of beneficence and non-maleficence derive historically from the doctor-patient relationship, which for centuries was based on paternalism. In the last few decades, there has been a change in the doctor-patient relationship involving a move towards greater respect for patients' autonomy, in that patients play a more active role in making decisions about their own treatment. According to [theologian Grace] Kao, this is not the same in non-Western medicine. She explains that in Islamic medical ethics, a greater emphasis is placed on beneficence than on autonomy especially at the time of death. [Ethicists Sahin] Aksoy and [Ali] Tenik, who investigated the existence of the four principles in the Islamic tradition by examining the works of Mawlana, a prominent Sufi theologian and philosopher, support this claim. They found evidence of all four principles in one form or another, with a clear emphasis on the principle of beneficence. In China where medical ethics were greatly influenced by Confucianism [referring to ethics based on the teachings of Confucius, a Chinese philosopher], there is also a great emphasis on beneficence in that Chinese medicine is considered "a humane art, and a physician must be loving in order to treat the sick and heal the injured," [in Kao's words].

The Principle of Justice

The principle of justice could be described as the moral obligation to act on the basis of fair adjudication between competing claims. As such, it is linked to fairness, entitlement and equality. In health care ethics, this can be subdivided into three categories: fair distribution of scarce resources (distributive justice), respect for people's rights (rights-based justice) and respect for morally acceptable laws (legal justice). [Dr. Annick] Alperovitch [and his colleagues] describe two elements of the principle of justice, namely equality and equity.

The right to be treated equally, and in some cases equal access to treatment, can be found in many constitutions, but in actual practice, a number of different factors may influence actual access to treatment, e.g., age, place of residence, social status, ethnic background, culture, sexual preferences, disability, legal capacity, hospital budgets, insurance cover and prognosis. The Swiss Academy of Medical Sciences recently reported that doctors and other medical staff are increasingly refusing to administer potentially useful treatment for economic reasons and there has been considerable debate in the UK [United Kingdom] over the refusal of expensive treatment to patients who would benefit from it.

Justice is more than mere equality in that people can be treated unjustly even if they are treated equally.

With regard to equality in the provision of care, some people are not treated with the same degree of respect as that accorded to others, e.g., with indifference, unfriendliness, lack of concern or rudeness. Such attitudes, prejudice and discrimination may, in some cases, be a reflection of the stigmatization of people belonging to groups identified and devalued on the basis of a particular attribute (of which dementia is one example). Inequality and discrimination may also be based on structural violence such as racism, sexism and poverty, which [ethicist Eugene] Kelly describes as a form of discrimination based on unequal power relations.

[Ethicist Raanan] Gillon emphasises that justice is more than mere equality in that people can be treated unjustly even if they are treated equally. With reference to [Greek philosopher] Aristotle, he argues that it is important to treat equals equally and unequals unequally in proportion to the morally relevant inequalities (the criterion for which is still being debated). Situations will always arise where decisions have to be taken and there are limited resources, different options and/or other conflicting moral concerns. Care must be taken to ensure that health care resources are used sensibly and fairly. People with dementia are potentially vulnerable in that they are likely at some stage to be unable to state their preferences and ensure that they are respected. Advance directives at least provide written evidence of their wishes, which should go some way towards ensuring that they are not placed at a disadvantage to others when it comes to making crucial decisions about their health and well-being. Health care proxies could also play a useful role in ensuring that such decisions are taken into account and, as far as possible, respected.

Nevertheless, it is possible that a high degree of incapacity and increased vulnerability, perhaps combined with failure by others to recognise their personhood, may result in a lack of distributive justice.

The Vatican Outlines Biomedical Ethics

Julia Duin

In the following viewpoint, religion writer and assistant national editor for the Washington Times *Julia Duin reports on* Dignitas Personae, *a statement of doctrine from the Catholic Church regarding ethical issues in medicine such as the treatment of fertilized embryos, fertility technologies, and human cloning. In most cases, the Vatican is opposed to fertility treatments—such as artificial insemination—as well as surrogate motherhood. Likewise, the freezing of fertilized embryos is not allowed under Vatican doctrine.*

As you read, consider the following questions:

1. What is in vitro fertilization?
2. How does the author describe selective reduction?
3. What is the Vatican's stance on the adoption of fertilized embryos by infertile couples?

Designer babies, human/animal hybrids, cloning, stem cell research and a whole range of common biomedical innovations are forbidden, the Vatican said Friday [December 12, 2008] in a document about procreation and genetic technologies.

But gene therapies, some fertility treatments and possibly embryo "adoption" are allowed, according to *Dignitas Perso-*

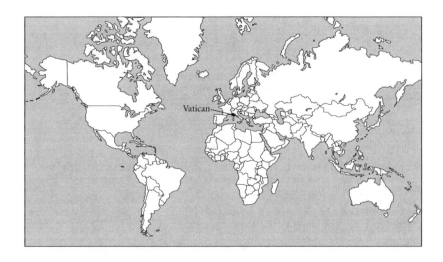

nae, a 32-page document. It was penned by Cardinal William J. Levada, the American who heads the Congregation for the Doctrine of the Faith, the Vatican's doctrinal arm, and his staff.

The title, which means "the dignity of a person" in Latin, stresses repeatedly why an embryo must be treated as a person even before implantation on the uterine wall. It merits "unconditional respect" from the moment of conception, which occurs as soon as an egg is fertilized, thus creating a genetically distinct individual.

[An embryo] merits "unconditional respect" from the moment of conception, which occurs as soon as an egg is fertilized, thus creating a genetically distinct individual.

Dignitas Personae updates a 1987 Vatican document, *Donum Vitae* [The Gift of Life], addressing biological innovations almost unknown 21 years ago: gene therapy, cloning, embryonic stem cell lines and the commercialization of frozen embryos. The document was released Friday morning; a copy was obtained by the *Washington Times*.

It also criticizes the "eugenic perspective" of many medical researchers, saying these scientists commit "injustice" by freezing or destroying a helpless embryo.

"It says, 'This is a person from the first moment,'" said the Rev. J. Daniel Mindling, a moral theologian at Mount St. Mary's Seminary in Emmitsburg, Md. "In pro-abortion rhetoric, people wanted to say the embryo only had rights at some later point because it was not a person yet."

Basic to the Catholic Church's concept of the individual is that the sexual act between a married couple brings that person into existence. The new person must be a "fruit of the conjugal act"; hence any fertility technologies that substitute for that—such as artificial insemination, surrogate motherhood and intracytoplasmic sperm injection—are forbidden, the document said.

In vitro fertilization, during which multiple eggs are taken from a woman's ovaries, fertilized, then frozen until implantation in the womb got specific condemnation, even though the document recognized that one-third of all women who try the procedure, succeed in conceiving.

"Given the proportion between total number of embryos produced and those eventually born, the number of embryos sacrificed is extremely high," the document said. Roughly 90 percent of all frozen embryos are discarded or die.

Each of these embryos is "deserving of full respect," it said, and not to be put in a freezer and withdrawn whenever a couple decides to have more children.

"In any other area of medicine, ordinary professional ethics and the health care authorities themselves would never allow a medical procedure which involved such a high number of failures and fatalities," the document said.

Freezing of fertilized embryos also was declared forbidden because of the high mortality rate of embryos that do not survive the freezing or thawing process. The Catholic Church considers these embryos to be human beings.

Use of these embryos for research is "unacceptable" because they are treated as "mere biological material" fit only for destruction, the document says.

The United States leads the world in stockpiling fertilized embryos. Based on a 2002 study by the RAND Corp., the number of frozen embryos in American fertility banks is estimated at 500,000. A 2005 study by the University of California at San Francisco says the average couple has seven remaining embryos left after a successful fertilization.

The answer to this, the Vatican says, is not to freeze embryos at all, as they deserve "to be protected by law as human persons."

The Vatican also addresses "selective reduction," whereby multiple embryos are placed in a woman's uterus in the hopes of at least one pregnancy. Often a woman becomes pregnant with multiple fetuses and aborts, or "reduces," one or more to make room for others in the womb.

This, the Vatican says, is still a condemned abortion, even if the goal is to raise the chances of viability for the remaining children.

"It is never permitted to do anything which is intrinsically illicit," the document said, "not even in view of a good result. The end does not justify the means."

Preimplantation diagnosis, whereby a fertilized embryo is searched for genetic defects before implantation in the womb, is also wrong, the Vatican said, because eliminating embryos with genetic defects, or simply being an unwanted sex, also constitutes abortion.

The Vatican had especially scathing language for people who tried this route, saying such diagnoses are part of a "eugenic mentality" that uses abortion to prevent the births of children with various anomalies.

Introduction to the *Dignitas Personae,* A Vatican Document on Bioethics

The dignity of a person must be recognized in every human being from conception to natural death. This fundamental principle expresses *a great "yes" to human life* and must be at the center of ethical reflection on biomedical research, which has an ever-greater importance in today's world. The Church's Magisterium [teach authority of the Church] has frequently intervened to clarify and resolve moral questions in this area. The instruction *Donum Vitae* [The Gift of Life] was particularly significant. And now [in September 2008], twenty years after its publication, it is appropriate to bring it up to date.

The teaching of *Donum Vitae* remains completely valid, both with regard to the principles on which it is based and the moral evaluations which it expresses. However, new biomedical technologies which have been introduced in the critical area of human life and the family have given rise to further questions, in particular in the field of research on human embryos, the use of stem cells for therapeutic purposes, as well as in other areas of experimental medicine. These new questions require answers. The pace of scientific developments in this area and the publicity they have received have raised expectations and concerns in large sectors of public opinion. Legislative assemblies have been asked to make decisions on these questions in order to regulate them by law; at times, wider popular consultation has also taken place.

Congregation for the Doctrine of the Faith, "Introduction,"
Instruction *Dignitas Personae* on Certain Bioethical Questions,
United States Conference of Catholic Bishops, September 8, 2008.
www.usccb.org.

"Such an attitude is shameful and utterly reprehensible," it said, "it . . . presumes to measure the value of a human life only within the parameters of 'normality' or physical well-being, thus opening the way to legitimizing infanticide and euthanasia as well."

The document also condemned human cloning, because it bypasses the sex act in creating a human being, including therapeutic cloning, which requires the destruction of human embryos.

Preimplantation diagnosis . . . is also wrong, the Vatican said, because eliminating embryos with genetic defects, or simply being an unwanted sex, also constitutes abortion.

"To create embryos with the intention of destroying them, even with the intention of helping the sick, is completely incompatible with human dignity," the document said, "because it makes the existence of a human being at the embryonic stage nothing more than a means to be used and destroyed."

It also tells Catholics not to use vaccines made from such stem cells or fetal tissue. Some of the popular vaccines for rubella, mumps and measles use material from abortions.

"They must be respected just as the remains of other human beings," the document said.

"They're saying we should raise a voice against society relying on tissue from aborted children for research and vaccines," said Richard Doerflinger, associate director for the U.S. Conference of Catholic Bishops secretariat of pro-life activities. "Some of the tissues from these vaccines are from an abortion that was procured 30 years ago."

The document did approve the therapeutic use of stem cells from adults, umbilical cord blood and children who have died in the womb of natural causes—but not from living embryos.

But aids to fertility—such as hormonal treatments, surgery on blocked fallopian tubes or for endometriosis—are licit. The document also approves gene therapies that seek to correct genetic defects, such as cystic fibrosis or Tay-Sachs disease, so as not to transmit disease to one's offspring.

But it forbids manipulating genes in an embryo, ovum or sperm to improve the gene pool, thus creating a "designer" child or a super race.

"Such manipulation would promote a eugenic mentality and would lead to indirect social stigma with regard to people who lack certain qualities," it said, "while privileging qualities that happen to be appreciated by a certain culture or society."

Left intentionally vague, some scholars said, is the question of embryo "adoption" for infertile couples.

The Church frowns on the procedure, because the child came from in vitro fertilization.

"It is a bit ambiguous," said Steve Bozza, who counsels such couples for the Diocese of Camden, N.J. "We need to get some bishops here to help us on this.

"I know of many good theologians who would say you're giving these embryos a chance for life. Others would argue against this. The document is probably leaving open the idea we can go this route. If they say no to it now, it will be difficult to change that."

Father Mindling said the document used the term "prenatal adoption" for these frozen embryos, putting the matter in terms of "rescuing" a doomed human being.

"The fact that this [document] does not explicitly rule out the option of prenatal adoption, but uses language that is ambiguous, does sound like it's inviting ethical speculation," he said. "Here are human persons who have rights and should be protected by law but are in this terrible situation."

In Australia, Medical Ethics Demand Acceptance of Cultural Diversity

David L. Bennett, Peter Chown, and Melissa S.-L. Kang

In the following viewpoint, David L. Bennett, Peter Chown, and Melissa S.-L. Kang argue that the great cultural diversity found in Australia has an impact on adolescents as they are maturing. This cultural diversity requires health care professionals to be sensitive to the needs of the young person in the context of their own culture beyond the physical complaint that has caused the young person to seek medical advice or help. It is important to be respectful and nonjudgmental of another's culture, while at the same time not assuming that culture is always an issue. The authors work at hospitals in Sydney, Australia. David L. Bennett is a physician in the Department of Adolescent Medicine at the Children's Hospital at Westmead. Peter Chown is a consultant at the NSW Centre for the Advancement of Adolescent Health, Department of General Practice, University of Sydney at Westmead Hospital. Melissa S.-L. Kang is a lecturer in the Department of General Practice, University of Sydney at Westmead Hospital.

As you read, consider the following questions:

1. According to the authors, what is the primary goal of the consultation with the adolescent?

David L. Bennett, Peter Chown, and Melissa S.-L. Kang, "Cultural Diversity in Adolescent Health Care," *MJA*, vol. 183, no. 8, 2005, pp. 436–438. Copyright © 2005 *The Medical Journal of Australia*. Reproduced with permission.

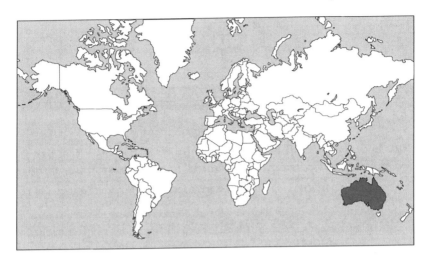

2. According to the authors, why is it important to engage the family when treating young people?
3. According to the authors, what should the physisican do if he/she encounters language difficulties with an adolescent?

Development is the unfolding of an individual's full potential in a given cultural context. "Adolescence" may be understood differently across cultures and, even within cultures, continues to evolve over time. [Note: The terms "adolescents" and "young people" are used interchangeably to refer to the age group 12–24 years.] While some cultures emphasise the importance of the individual and the achievement of independence, others tend to place greater value on ethnic identity and allegiance to family. In a multicultural society like Australia, where about 16% of young people are born overseas and 24% are from a non-English-speaking background, adolescent health care is inevitably a multicultural challenge. Furthermore, health professionals themselves are a culturally diverse group, adding to the rich interplay of cultures in interactions with adolescent patients and their families.

Adolescence and Culture

In Australia, some young people are dealing not only with the developmental tasks of adolescence but also the experience of growing up between two cultures. While young people's experience of belonging to or identifying with a particular culture can enhance their resilience and promote overall well-being, some adolescents not born in Australia may be at risk of poor mental health from stresses related to migration, resettlement and acculturation, as well as exposure to traumatic experiences.

Young people are generally reluctant to seek professional help for their concerns, and additional barriers to care can arise from a lack of confidence and skills among service providers. Where cultural differences exist between young people and their health care providers, there is the potential for misunderstanding. Health professionals need to be particularly sensitive to the cultural influences operating in an adolescent's life and have an appreciation of the wide range of cultural, ethnic, linguistic and social differences among adolescents.

Culturally Appropriate Consultation

Culture may be defined as "the shared, learned meanings and behaviours that are transmitted from within a social activity context for purposes of promoting individual/societal adjustment, growth and development". Thus, concepts of culture extend beyond language and ethnicity. Other factors such as age and generational issues, gender, sexuality, geographic location, religion and socioeconomic status may have as much or more cultural significance for any individual or community.

In dealing with young people from culturally diverse backgrounds, health care providers can function at a number of different levels. "Cultural awareness" is the recognition and acknowledgement that we are all "cultural beings" and that this may affect our interactions with adolescents, their families and our colleagues. "Cultural sensitivity" is the conscious attempt to understand the possible influences of culture and cultural differences on interactions between adolescents, their families and ourselves. "Cultural competency" is the ability to identify and challenge one's own cultural assumptions, values and beliefs, the development of empathy for people viewing the world through a different cultural lens, and the application of specific communication and interaction skills that can be learned and integrated into clinical encounters. There is a growing body of evidence to support the need for cultural competence among health professionals to positively influence clinical consultations and health outcomes.

"Cultural competency" is the ability to identify and challenge one's own cultural assumptions, values and beliefs, the development of empathy for people viewing the world through a different cultural lens.

Communicating Effectively

The primary goal of the consultation with an adolescent, regardless of the presenting complaint or cultural background, is to foster a relationship of trust. The skills required to communicate in a culturally appropriate manner are the same generic skills that apply to consultation with any adolescent— namely an open, sensitive, empathic and nonjudgmental approach; a positive regard and respect for differing values and practices; reassurance about confidentiality; an open-ended questioning style that avoids medical jargon; reassurance of normality; and the allaying of fears and anxieties.

Preliminary measures include creating a "culturally friendly" practice environment by providing multilingual pamphlets on different health topics, displaying multilingual posters, artefacts or photographs that reflect specific cultural groups, scheduling longer appointments with adolescents from culturally and linguistically different backgrounds, asking how they would like to be addressed and learning to pronounce their names correctly.

The psychosocial history is crucial, and should include questions that enquire into acculturation and identity issues. Examples include asking about ways in which they do or don't follow the norms of their culture; how they view themselves within the context of their culture; how they feel about their own culture, their parents' culture, and host culture; what has changed, if anything, since they reached adolescence; and whether they are now treated differently by parents, siblings, and relatives.

Adopt a respectful, open and nonjudgmental approach in dealing with differing cultural norms and practices. Be aware of your own cultural beliefs and values and the fact that these may not necessarily be aligned with those of a young person from a different cultural background. Assumptions about the role of verbal and nonverbal behaviour (such as eye contact) may not be transferable from one culture to another. Be mindful that it may be culturally unacceptable for a young person to discuss "private" family matters or to talk openly about his or her feelings.

Finally, avoid cultural stereotyping. People from a particular cultural or language background may not share the same set of cultural attributes, beliefs and practices, and it cannot be assumed that the young person necessarily relates to the cultural identity of the parents. . . .

Assumptions about the role of verbal and nonverbal behaviour (such as eye contact) may not be transferable from one culture to another.

Exploring Cultural Issues Around Diagnosis and Treatment

While it is important to assess the degree to which cultural factors may play a role in diagnosis and treatment, do not assume that culture is always an issue.

- Ask about the meaning of a young person's symptoms, where relevant, within the context of their culture of origin (e.g., mental health symptoms related to depression, anxiety or eating disorders).

- Ask sensitively about experiences that may have adversely affected their development, health and attitudes to illness (e.g., refugee experience, exposure to war and trauma, discrimination, racism). Be aware that the young person may be especially reticent about discussing these experiences.

- Learn whether cultural difference (e.g., attitudes to sexuality) might affect treatment.

- Be sensitive to gender issues, particularly the needs of young women, when conducting physical examinations or investigating sexual health problems. Where possible, provide a female practitioner, or offer to conduct the examination in the presence of a female nurse or family member (if acceptable to the young person).

- Develop a management plan that considers the influence of cultural issues and is culturally acceptable.

Engaging the Family

Engaging the family and gaining the trust of parents is critical in treating young people from other cultures. In many cultures, participation in health care is a family responsibility rather than an individual responsibility.

- Respect parents' authority with regard to decision making, while helping them to understand their child's growing need for independence appropriate to his or her age and stage of development.

- Where the young person is accompanied by a parent, try to spend some time alone with the adolescent. Explain to the parents your reasons for doing this and seek their permission.

- Where appropriate, engage the support and involvement of parents and family in treatment, but never use a family member as interpreter (see next section).

Dealing with Language Difficulties

Given the linguistically diverse nature of health professionals, language may not be an issue in consultations with culturally and linguistically diverse young people and their families. It may not be a problem even when dealing with people from a cultural background different to that of the health care provider. However, where there are language difficulties, use a professional health care interpreter. Do not rely on a member of the family, who may also have limited English and/or have an interest in presenting his or her own point of view. Even when a child or teenager is the most language-competent person in the family, many problems (ethical, cultural, informational, familial) can occur if the child is used in this way.

Also be aware of medicolegal issues—consent can only be given by a patient or parents if they are properly informed, which includes understanding the language used.

Irrespective of whether or not language is an issue, check out whether the young person and parents have clearly understood the questions asked and the information given to them. For example, check their understanding of the diagnosis and treatment instructions by asking them to repeat the instructions back to you in their own words. Do not assume that they have understood just because they say they have—in some cultures it may be considered impolite to disagree with or question an older person or someone in authority.

In framing questions for people who are functionally competent in English but not sophisticated speakers, consider the

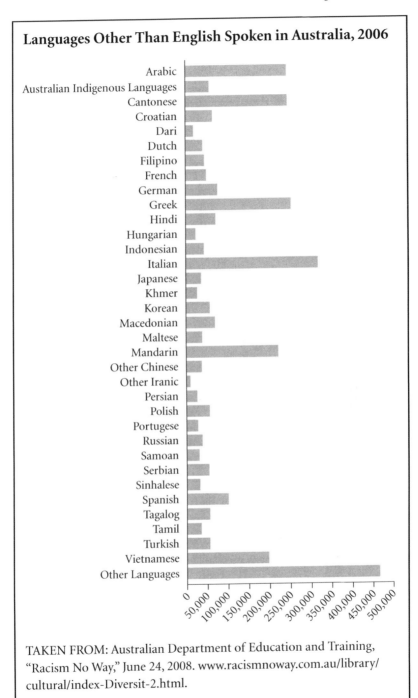

Languages Other Than English Spoken in Australia, 2006

TAKEN FROM: Australian Department of Education and Training, "Racism No Way," June 24, 2008. www.racismnoway.com.au/library/ cultural/index-Diversit-2.html.

importance of volume, clarity and pace of speech (speak slowly); use of simple, nontechnical language (of benefit to all patients); avoiding idioms or slang; nonverbal behaviour (e.g., importance of nonverbal indicators of respect); questioning and clarifying; and the use of open-ended questions. . . .

Irrespective of whether or not language is an issue, check out whether the young person and parents have clearly understood the questions asked and the information given to them.

Conclusion

Diversity among adolescent patients represents a significant challenge for the medical profession. The integral relationships between culture, development and health, and the expertise required by health practitioners to provide a culturally appropriate service, play out in adolescent practice. While cultural competence training has been shown to improve the knowledge, attitudes and skills of health professionals, we should continue to seek better ways of improving health outcomes and patient adherence to therapy.

Meanwhile, an approach that incorporates respect for young people as individuals within their cultural framework, as well as sensitivity to the issues they and their families may face as migrants or refugees settling in a new country, will go a long way towards ensuring that they receive appropriate and effective health care.

VIEWPOINT

In India, Some Medical Professionals Are Not Ethical

Vijay Mahajan

In the following viewpoint, Vijay Mahajan asserts that although criminal medical doctors in India are a minority, their numbers are increasing. Mahajan cites cases where doctors ignore their medical ethics in the quest for more money. He also holds the Indian government responsible for not adequately funding public health. In addition, he singles out the trade in human organs as particularly unethical. Mahajan closes the viewpoint with a to-do list for cleaning up the medical profession. Mahajan is a professor of medicine at Panjab University.

As you read, consider the following questions:

1. What are some ways corruption surfaces in medical colleges, according to Mahajan?
2. What percentage of its gross national product does India spend on health, according to the viewpoint?
3. What are six things doctors must do to defeat corruption, according to Mahajan?

India is said to have one of the most corrupt medical systems in the world. The situation has become so bad that patients today approach the doctor with mixed feelings—of

Indian Journal of Medical Ethics, vol. 7, no. 1, January–March 2010, for "White Coated Corruption," by Vijay Mahajan. Reproduced by permission of the publisher and author.

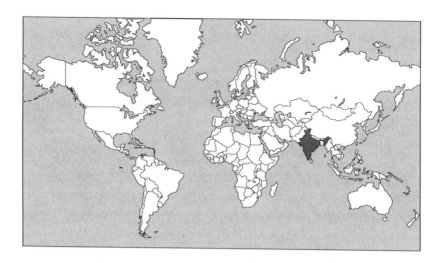

faith and fear, of hope and hostility. This leads to a distorted doctor-patient relationship, with high chances of exploitation both ways—doctors may fleece patients and, if some lacunae are exposed in treatment, patients or their relatives may blackmail doctors.

Such unethical practices may no longer be cause for comment. But there are many reports of doctors actually committing crimes—distorting medical reports in medicolegal cases, providing false certificates to protect criminals, sexually assaulting their patients, and even trading in human organs.

It goes without saying that such criminal doctors are in a minority. Unfortunately their number seems to be increasing.

Inhumane Doctors

One can quote innumerable reports pointing to the inhumanity of persons in white coats. Pregnant women have been refused care because they are HIV [human immunodeficiency virus] positive. Hospital authorities have refused to release the bodies of patients who died in their care because the relatives could not afford to pay the medical bills. There are reports of doctors amputating the limbs of poor people at the bidding of the begging mafia. Poor people who resisted the extraction of their kidneys have reportedly been operated upon at gun-point. The list of such practices is endless.

It starts in medical college as MBBS [bachelor of medicine and bachelor of surgery] seats are sold for lakhs of rupees [large sums of money]. This is merely the tip of the iceberg. Rampant corruption exists at every level, from medical college admissions, getting a degree, to registration with the medical council. Question papers have been leaked and "jockeys" have written medical examinations on behalf of students. Medical college managements are known to charge unofficial "dona-tions" in addition to official fees. Students have been reported to bribe faculty to get good reports, and doctors have been re-ported to pay bribes to get registered with the state medical council.

There are many reports of doctors actually committing crimes—distorting medical reports in medicolegal cases, providing false certificates to protect criminals, sexually assaulting their patients, and even trading in human or-gans.

New graduates quickly learn the rules of the game in gov-ernment service. Within medical administrations, lucrative posts are sold to the highest bidder. Government vehicles and machinery are misused. Pharmacists perform the duties of doctors in government dispensaries. Medical supplies get di-verted from the intended users. Health officers serve VIPs in order to benefit from their proximity to the powerful. Govern-ment doctors pay more attention to their private practice de-spite receiving non-practising allowances. They do not attend rural postings despite drawing wages from the government. Patients are forced to bribe everyone in the hospital hierarchy to get the medical treatment that is their right.

Making Money Is the Only Goal

Private medical services are no better. Though medical professionals are expected to work in the interests of the public in general and of the poor in particular, all of us know that this does not always happen in practice. There are some doctors for whom making money is the only goal.

So, spurious and adulterated drugs proliferate, and licensing, accreditation and regulatory systems are subverted. Pharmacists sell their licenses to unqualified persons to run chemist shops. Even in the big cities, quacks practice without registration. Sex determination tests are performed though they are illegal. Doctors are known to prescribe unnecessary diagnostic tests, hazardous drugs and inappropriate surgical procedures, all for the kickbacks they receive from the health care industry. The avenues for corruption are endless.

Medical establishments work closely with drug manufacturers whose main objective is to maximise profits. Large quantities of drugs must be sold, and for this, anything goes. Doctors are the principal salespeople of drug companies and they are rewarded with research grants, gifts, lavish perquisites and foreign tours. The principal buyers are the public, who must be thoroughly medicated and vaccinated at any cost.

The Government Is Also Responsible

Though India is a welfare state, the role of the government at the centre and in the states in providing health care facilities is deplorable. Against the recommendations of the WHO [World Health Organization] that the total health expenditure should be 6.5% of the gross national product (GNP), India spends only 4.8% of GNP on health. Further, public health expenditure is just 1.2% of GNP, or barely 25% of the total health expenditure; the rest of the money is paid by patients directly to private doctors and hospitals for whom profits may take precedence over their patients' interests.

Even in government hospitals, medical facilities favour the well-to-do and are often beyond the reach of the poor who need them the most. The allocation of funds is often determined by the influence and manipulations of hospital authorities, and the maintenance of government hospitals is poor. Public funding for research and development is inadequate and whatever meagre resources are available may actually be used by people at the top to serve their own interests.

The Connivance of Regulators

The dubious functioning of regulatory bodies of the medical profession, namely the Medical Council of India (MCI) and the Indian Medical Association (IMA), has helped spread corruption in the profession. What can we expect if the president of the MCI, who also happens to be head of the IMA, must be removed from his post after being found guilty of dishonest practices and misuse of power?

Large amounts of money can be involved in getting the MCI's approval for setting up a private medical college. Even government medical colleges and hospitals go on reckless spending sprees before an MCI inspection. As medical and nursing colleges are income-generating ventures, their owners readily offer huge bribes to the officials who matter in the establishment of such institutions.

By the 1990s, India had achieved the distinction of being the biggest bazaar for the sale of human organs and the sale of kidneys was described as a cottage industry in India.

Unfortunately, we cannot rely on justice from the legal system. When prosecutions do occur, only a small fraction of these cases reaches the courts. In some cases of medical negligence, the punishment has been notional. Many cases of medical negligence are pending in various courts in the country; in the Supreme Court of India alone, there are some 3,000 cases of medical negligence.

By the 1990s, India had achieved the distinction of being the biggest bazaar for the sale of human organs and the sale of kidneys was described as a cottage industry in India. Such scandals prompted the government of India to enact the Transplantation of Human Organs Act, 1994, but the nexus of doctors and brokers involved in the sale of human organs has never been afraid of the law, which has been violated with impunity. For example, the Gurgaon kidney scamsters, who had been arrested for conducting illegal kidney transplants in the 1990s, evaded punishment and managed to run their trade in kidneys for years, obviously with the connivance of law enforcement authorities. It is known that the man accused evaded arrest by bribing Delhi police officials.

Poverty and Public Ignorance

The nexus between corrupt medical professionals and politicians, bureaucrats and the police is one of the major factors multiplying medical corruption. The common man is afraid of exposing wrongdoings—the authorities may hush up the matter and target the whistleblower instead.

Public apathy and fear are also partly responsible for breeding medical corruption. Even if people come to know about unethical and illegal activities in the profession, they turn a blind eye, either because it does not concern them, or because they are afraid of the doctors. For example, many people were aware of the kidney racket but did not report the matter to law enforcing agencies fearing the consequences to themselves.

The organ trade has been fuelled by poverty; poverty drives people to fall into the trap set by unscrupulous elements who lure them with offers of money and jobs in exchange for a kidney. At the same time, voluntary donation of human or-

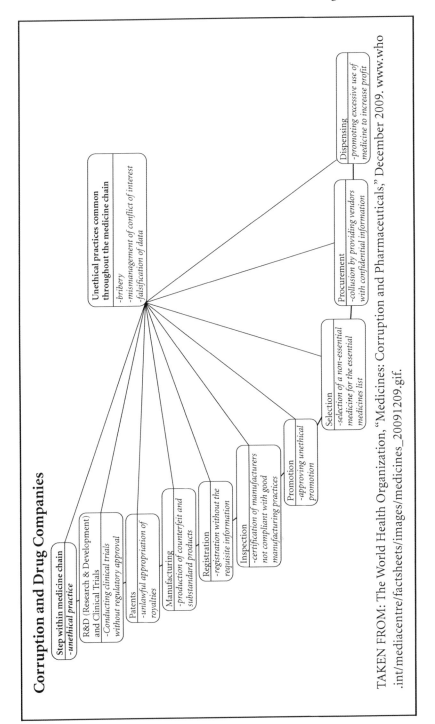

Corruption and Drug Companies

| Step within medicine chain |
| -*unethical practice* |

R&D (Research & Development) and Clinical Trials
-*Conducting clinical trials without regulatory approval*

Patents
-*unlawful appropriation of royalties*

Manufacturing
-*production of counterfeit and substandard products*

Registration
-*registration without the requisite information*

Inspection
-*certification of manufacturers not compliant with good manufacturing practices*

Promotion
-*approving unethical promotion*

Selection
-*selection of a non-essential medicine for the essential medicines list*

Procurement
-*collusion by providing vendors with confidential information*

Dispensing
-*promoting excessive use of medicine to increase profit*

Unethical practices common throughout the medicine chain
-*bribery*
-*mismanagement of conflict of interest*
-*falsification of data*

TAKEN FROM: The World Health Organization, "Medicines: Corruption and Pharmaceuticals," December 2009. www.who.int/mediacentre/factsheets/images/medicines_20091209.gif.

gans is not properly promoted or utilised because of poor hospital infrastructures, inefficient transportation systems for the timely revival of organs, and a shortage of cadaveric transplant surgeons. Because of the shortage of cadaver donors, doctors, donors and patients waiting for transplants collude in illegal practices.

Social compulsions accelerate the process of medical corruption. A medical professional finds it very difficult to refuse a VIP's request; it could mean isolation or posting to a remote area. When honest doctors cannot afford to even buy their own houses, but see that their dishonest colleagues enjoy a luxurious life, they may wonder if they are right to stick to their principles.

How to Clean Up the Medical Profession

It is not too late to restrain the medical profession. This calls for a well-coordinated campaign involving doctors, the government and the public. A beginning has to be made by health professionals launching a zero tolerance assault on medical corruption. The MCI code has to be practised in letter and spirit.

The list of things that doctors must do is long. A few of them are given below.

- Refuse to take bribes.

- Collectively publicly oppose outside interference—political, bureaucratic or otherwise.

- Make a commitment to rational drug use, referral and evidence-based interventions.

- Shun erring colleagues.

- Refuse to accept any favours from pharmaceutical companies.

- Follow medical ethics and treat poor patients the same as rich ones.

The government must support and protect the interests of upright doctors. For this, it must take the following steps:

- Evolve a transparent system for the allocation of funds, for deciding the location of medical facilities and for the posting of medical personnel; this system must be insulated from political and other interference.

- Have people of integrity conduct prompt enquiries into reports of medical corruption, and take prompt action on the basis of these reports.

- Let doctors know that transgressions will be met with punishment. Medical corruption is not a crime committed in the heat of the moment. It is calculated and based on greed, and the punishment must be severe and deterrent.

- Plug the loopholes in the law on human organ transplants that enable transplant tourism and marriages for the purposes of kidney "donation". A campaign must be started to dispel myths on cadaveric donations. The transplant programme must include a computerized national database, efficient transportation and a network of state-of-the-art transplantation centres with expert surgeons.

- Reward upright doctors to encourage role models for new entrants in the profession.

- Tackle the problem of doctors shunning government service.

- Support and protect whistleblowers who report medical corruption.

- Form a task force to defend high ethical standards in the medical profession and to fight corruption in public health care.

Medical corruption contributes to poverty and misery in a developing country like India. The public must contribute to efforts made by medical professionals and the government to clean up the medical system. It can do this by:

- acting as a watchdog reporting corruption or wrong doing;

- checking unscrupulous elements who blackmail doctors in cases of inadvertent lapses in medical treatment;

To restore [the medical system's] noble and distinct status, all sections of society must work together to stamp out the biggest killer in the medical system—corruption.

- being more responsive to the stress that doctors have to deal with, and

- running awareness groups to educate people on the necessity of organ donation and to encourage the framing of laws that would empower medical authorities to extract organs of unidentified and unclaimed dead bodies within the stipulated time for organ revival.

Corruption is spreading its tentacles far and wide in the medical system. To restore its noble and distinct status, all sections of society must work together to stamp out the biggest killer in the medical system—corruption.

Periodical and Internet Sources Bibliography

The following articles have been selected to supplement the diverse views presented in this chapter.

Owen Beattie et al.	"Ethical Issues in Resolving the Organ Shortage: The Views of Recent Immigrants and Healthcare Professionals," *Health Law Review*, March 22, 2010.
Peter Bowen-Simpkins	"Should We Impose an Age Limit on IVF?" *Times* (UK), May 29, 2009.
Madeleine Brindley	"MMR Controversy Doctor Found to Be 'Irresponsible,'" *Western Mail* (Wales), January 29, 2010.
Cathy Lynn Grossman	"Medical, Religious Ethics Often Are a Tug-of-War," *USA Today*, June 8, 2010.
Bebe Loff	"World Trade, the Poor and Swine Flu," *Indian Journal of Medical Ethics*, vol. 7, no. 1, January–March 2010.
Ofer Merin et al.	"The Israeli Field Hospital in Haiti—Ethical Dilemmas in Early Disaster Response," *New England Journal of Medicine*, March 18, 2010.
Govind Persad, Alan Wertheimer, and Ezekiel J. Emanuel	"Principles for Allocation of Scarce Medical Interventions," *Lancet*, vol. 373, no. 9661, January 2009.
Jim Rutenberg	"In Health Care Debate, Bioethicist Becomes a Lightning Rod for Criticism," *New York Times*, August 25, 2009.
Margaret Somerville	"A World of Competing Sorrows," *Globe and Mail* (Canada), July 15, 2009.
Marcel Verweij	"Moral Principles for Allocating Scarce Medical Resources in an Influenza Pandemic," *Journal of Bioethical Inquiry*, vol. 6, no. 2, May 2009.

GLOBALVIEWPOINTS

CHAPTER 2

Medical Ethics and the End of Life

In India, Palliative Care Follows Ethical Guidelines

Bidhu K. Mohanti

In the following viewpoint, Bidhu K. Mohanti reviews the foundation of medical ethics in India, including autonomy, beneficence, non-maleficence, justice, dignity, truthfulness, and honesty. He argues that palliative care is compatible with these ethical guidelines. He also argues that palliative care and the relief of pain is both a legal and ethical choice as well as a basic human right for late-stage cancer patients. The use of ethical standards complemented by palliative care, according to Mohanti, "maximizes the protection and satisfaction available to the vulnerable patient and family members." Mohanti is a professor of radiation oncology at the Dr. B.R.A. Institute Rotary Cancer Hospital in New Delhi, India.

As you read, consider the following questions:

1. Who betrayed scientific medicine's ideals, according to Mohanti? How and when did they do so?
2. Why does the public fear drugs such as sedatives and opioids, according to Mohanti?
3. What are four unique situations regarding the inclusion of patients in palliative care research?

Bidhu K. Mohanti, "Ethics in Palliative Care," *Indian Journal of Palliative Care*, vol. 15, no. 2, 2009, pp. 89–92. Copyright © 2005–2009 Medknow Publications Pvt. Ltd., India. All rights reserved. Reproduced by permission.

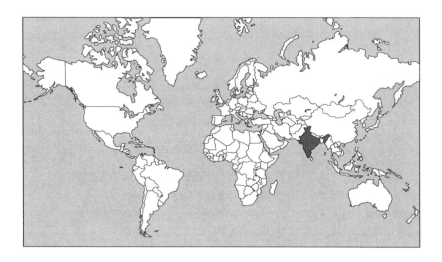

Physicians and nurses encounter difficulties in their practice of palliative care. They do need a good understanding of ethical principles and precedents.

> A 60-year-old lady with relapsed ovarian cancer, with ascites and profound dyspnea, is in her terminal stage of disease. She has this disease progression one year after her surgery and six months after chemotherapy. Her husband is a re-tired 65-year-old teacher with chronic heart disease. The son and daughter stay at distant places and can only visit frequently.

A good understanding of medical ethics will contribute to the health professional's decision making and day-to-day practice of medicine for a terminally ill patient.

There are a wide range of medical issues and ethical dilemmas that arise in the provision of palliative care for this lady. It is now realized that a good understanding of medical ethics will contribute to the health professional's decision making and day-to-day practice of medicine for a terminally ill patient.

The History of Medical Ethics

Medical ethics is primarily a field of applied ethics, the study of moral values and judgments as they apply to medicine. It is intended to provide guidelines and codes for physicians as for their *duty, responsibility* and *conduct* and shares many principles with other health care ethics, such as nursing ethics and bioethics. Historically, it can be traced back to Hippocrates, the ancient Greek physician of 4th century BC. Hippocrates (460–380 BC) and his school of students set themselves apart from other healers of their time by stressing that their professional pursuits were rational and scientific rather than magical or religious. Several medical thinkers have emphasized that a physician should carry 'a good sense and discretion'.

From the 18th century onwards, medical practitioners adopted the Hippocratic Oath as the rite of passage. Similarly, the guiding principle of nursing profession is known as Nightingale Pledge [named after Florence Nightingale, an English nurse]. These two, for the medical and nursing profession respectively, are enshrined in part as, 'I will prescribe regimens for the good of my patients according to my ability and my judgment and never do harm to anyone', and 'I will practice my profession with conscience and dignity'.

Major evolution and developments in medical ethics were made [in the] 20th century. The betrayal of scientific medicine's ideals during the Second World War by Nazi doctors, in carrying out inhuman medical practices amounting to torture and killing of innocent prisoners, lead to the Nuremberg trial in 1947. The Nuremberg code was issued and this is considered the basis of modern medical ethics. Treatment of human subjects, informed consent, protecting research subjects from harmful medical experiments were incorporated as laws of the society. These laws and policies are provided by Declaration of Geneva (1948, last modified in 2006) and further incorporated in Declaration of Helsinki (1964, last modi-

81

fied in October 2008). It is the responsibility of all medical practitioners to read these documents and imbibe the stated values.

Six Values in Medical Ethics

The foundation of medical ethics is supported by four pillars, namely:

- *Autonomy*—Patient has the right to choose or refuse the treatment.

- *Beneficence*—A doctor should act in the best interest of the patient.

- *Non-maleficence*—First, do no harm.

- *Justice*—It concerns the distribution of health resources equitably.

Added to the above four, are two more aspects which form the cornerstones of medical practice:

- *Dignity*—The patient and the persons treating the patient have the right to dignity.

- *Truthfulness and honesty*—The concept of informed consent and truth telling.

All these together constitute the six values of medical ethics.

Palliative Care and Medical Ethics

The lady with ovarian cancer, narrated at the beginning (who had earlier been treated by chemotherapy) could be offered second-line of aggressive chemotherapy. Is this the only option? Often the treating oncology team may be reluctant to discuss the *risk/benefit* aspects of second-line and may not consider the option of palliative care in the face of progressive ascites and pleural effusion.

This exemplifies the need for patient's autonomy, beneficence vs. non-maleficence, and truth telling. It is pertinent to understand the clinical decision-making process of 'withholding or withdrawing a treatment' (in this case the second-line chemotherapy with negligible response). Ezekiel [Emanuel] of the Bioethics Department, NIH [National Institutes of Health] USA, has expressed concerns about the quality of care that cancer patients get, 'physicians give patients, who are not responding, different aggressive therapy, "Just to try something." That is just not bad medicine, it is seriously unethical'.

It is known that the timely institution of palliative care alleviates the distressing symptoms in terminal stages of diseases, avoids toxicities of questionable anti-cancer therapy, and improves the quality of remaining life. The treating palliative care team may face conflicts in terms of patient's family carer refusing to stop the toxic anti-cancer therapy. Hence effective communication (and explanation of the disease process) is the key to ethical palliative care.

The Patient's Right to Know

The team should be knowledgeable to give proactive care, understand the patient's preferences and forgive conflicts. The process of truth telling in advanced cancer or any other terminal illness can be a difficult task. Whenever a patient is too moribund and not in a suitable mental stage, the family carers are required to give informed consent. The doctor and nurse in the palliative care team have to build the communication with a responsible family carer so that confidentiality and dignity for patient's last stage are maintained. Communication is meant to deal with ethical questions regarding two fundamental aspects of palliative care: to explain the concept of a good death and to resolve the conflicting needs of patient vis-à-vis family.

The lady with progressive ovarian cancer has fluid in abdomen and chest, and may not get a regular appetite. The

India Must Increase Access to Palliative Care

The right to health also requires a rational and equitable distribution of resources for health care services, based on the health needs of the population. The Indian government, however, while investing considerable resources into cancer and HIV [human immunodeficiency virus] services, has failed to make effective provisions of palliative care, even though the need for such services is extremely high.

Under the prohibition of torture and ill treatment, the Indian government has a positive obligation to take measures to protect people under its jurisdiction from inhuman or degrading treatment such as unnecessarily suffering from extreme pain. As the UN [United Nations] special rapporteur on torture and other cruel, inhuman or degrading treatment or punishment has noted, "failure of governments to take reasonable measures to ensure accessibility of pain treatment . . . raises questions whether they have adequately discharged this obligation." The fact that many of the government-designated regional cancer centers in India, which treat very large numbers of patients who require palliative care, do not offer it, do not stock morphine, and do not have health care workers on staff who have been trained in palliative care, strongly suggests that the Indian government has not taken any such reasonable measures. . . .

In order to end this unnecessary suffering, the Indian government will need to recognize the urgency of the problem and take proactive steps. . . .

Human Rights Watch, Unbearable Pain: India's Obligation to Ensure Palliative Care, *October 2009. www.hrw.org.*

husband could feel distressed that she is going to die in hunger. This needs a good explanation to alleviate the conflict regarding forced feeding in a terminal stage of cancer. Effective and compassionate communications are the integral components of ethics in palliative care.

For ethical reasons, the correct step would be to view pain as a public health crisis, and take the necessary steps to remove all hurdles [from the relief of pain].

Accessing Resources for Palliative Care

Pain is the dominant symptom for many advanced stage cancer patients and so also for other chronic illness like HIV/ AIDS [human immunodeficiency virus/acquired immune deficiency syndrome]. Pain can make a patient fearful, withdrawn, and agitated, and unrelieved pain leads to a miserable death leaving the family members remorseful in grief. Pain relief is successfully achieved by the scientific and holistic principles of analgesic [pain management] ladder in palliative care. Whereas relief of pain is a core ethical duty in medicine, it is observed that pain is the most neglected aspect in medical care. There are several interlinked causes for this neglect. Lack of knowledge and skill in pain assessment, improper medication, unavailability of morphine, unfounded myths about opioid addiction and sedation are some of the complex hurdles. The efforts of the World Health Organization (WHO) and various national bodies/associations of palliative care improved the situation. It is now recognized in most countries that relief from pain is a legal right and availability of morphine is a societal responsibility. For ethical reasons, the correct step would be to view pain as a public health crisis, and take the necessary steps to remove all hurdles.

The public fears that drugs such as sedatives and opioids prescribed in the terminal stage of a patient hasten the death process. The competent medical practitioners should dispel this myth. It is ethical to prescribe narcotics and sedatives for intractable pain, even when there is the possibility of *terminal sedation*. Such a possibility is called 'double effect' and the treating team should explain this aspect to the family members. Often metaphors can be highly effective, 'we had a patient with lung cancer who suffered from breathing difficulty and pain; he was constantly breathless, could not lie down, and did not sleep for nights together. Morphine calmed him down; he felt relieved, could sleep soundly, and passed away peacefully after two weeks. His wife felt a sense of relief when he could sleep well'.

End-of-life care is both a medical and an ethical challenge. Patients and their families can face several uncertainties. In the last part of life, with multiple distressing symptoms, infection, anorexia-cachexia [failure to take food or fluids], fatigue, mental confusion, etc., deciding the right place of care is the first priority. Whenever possible, a good death is when it comes at the patient's home, surrounded by family members and relatives. Hence, *advance care planning* should be recorded. As far as possible, home care instead of hospital or hospice should be explained by the palliative care team. In India, home care will be less expensive and a more practical approach to offer palliative care at the doorstep. There can crop up certain contentious issues like use of antibiotics, supportive drugs, blood transfusion, naso-gastric tube, parenteral nutrition, intensive care, etc. Wherever possible, the patient's preferences should be balanced with palliative care principles. Advance directives in the form of recording the patient's or family's consent should be routinely practiced. This will avoid the terminal palliative care patient being subjected to unnecessary tests, hospitalization, intensive monitoring, and resuscitation procedure. In many countries of the world, do-not-resuscitate (DNR) policy is well founded in end-of-life care. Of course, this is not yet a routine in India.

Palliative Care Is a Legal Choice

Legal aspects and human rights give the fundamental protections that allow equal participation and individual justice in a society. It means 'no one ought to harm another in his life, health, liberty or possessions'. In the 20th century, the right to health care is well established, encompassing not only the delivery of basic clinical services but also an environment that allows good health to flourish. In this context, a terminal stage patient (or even family member) may often seek to end his/her life. Euthanasia is defined as 'a deliberate intervention undertaken with the express intention of ending life to relieve intractable suffering'. The practice of euthanasia is legalized in some countries (the Netherlands, Belgium, some states of USA and Australia). However, euthanasia poses an ethical dilemma in palliative care. Simply said, 'a doctor or nurse is not trained to deliberately end a patient's life'. It is interesting to note that the spread of palliative care, use of analgesics, and effective prescription of terminal sedation (even in the face of double effect) have reduced the need for euthanasia, in a recent Dutch study. Hence, palliative care should be considered a better legal choice for the medical fraternity and the society.

The Ethical Challenges of Palliative Care Research

Good medical practice requires evidence of effectiveness to address deficits in care. There are substantial opportunities to improve palliative care. However, a treating physician can face dilemmas, because research that involves patients near the end of life creates numerous ethical challenges. Some of these dilemmas and challenges are real and some are perceived.

Inclusion of patients for palliative care research involves unique situations:

1. Dying patients are especially vulnerable.

2. Adequate informed consent may be difficult to obtain.

3. Balancing research and clinical roles is particularly difficult.

4. Risks and benefits of palliative care research are difficult
to assess.

In practice, the dying of an incurable patient is medically
recognized as a natural process. The patient can experience
dynamic changes in physical and psychosocial symptoms. It is
observed that there is prevalence of unrelieved symptoms such
as pain, fatigue, dyspnea, constipation/bowel obstruction,
depression/confusion and insomnia. Much progress has been
made in understanding and caring for most of these, yet
greater research focus is still needed in many areas. Palliative
care physicians and nurses should address existing deficits.
Balancing the ethical principles in terms protecting the vulnerable patient from harm and at the same time carrying out
scientifically designed studies should be possible.

---

*Suffering due to unrelieved pain and unavailability of
morphine are recognized as negligence of human rights.*

Medical Ethics and Palliative Care
Are Compatible

Palliative care is mandated in advanced stage incurable cancer
and other terminal chronic illnesses. The different aspects of
palliative care such as pain and symptom control, psychosocial
care, and end-of-life issues should be managed in an ethical
manner. The cardinal ethical principles to be followed are autonomy, beneficence, non-maleficence and justice. The palliative care experts and team members should carry out their responsibilities with honesty and dignity. Suffering due to
unrelieved pain and unavailability of morphine are recognized
as negligence of human rights. There are practical ethical
challenges which need to be resolved. Truth telling, place of
care, continuity of effective palliative care till the last days of

life, confidentiality, use of antibiotics and blood transfusion, nutrition and advance directives can be the key points which confront a palliative care team. Progress in palliative care will come out of good research and medical professionals should undertake trials and studies in a legal and ethical manner. The delivery of palliative care and medical ethics are complementary, and use of the two together maximizes the protection and satisfaction available to the vulnerable patient and family members.

In Ireland, Ethical Debate on Euthanasia Is Banned

Len Doyal

In the following viewpoint, Len Doyal argues that his views on euthanasia have the right to be heard. He asserts that although doctor-assisted euthanasia is illegal in Ireland, doctors routinely shorten lives by either not providing, or even withdrawing, life-sustaining treatments. He argues that doctors ought to be able to fulfill their promise to minimize suffering, even if this includes hastening death. He concludes that the topic of euthanasia ought to be open to free debate in Ireland. Doyal is emeritus professor of medical ethics at Queen Mary, University of London, and professor of public health and health services research at the University of East Anglia.

As you read, consider the following questions:

1. On what does Doyal assert his views on euthanasia are based?
2. On what grounds does Doyal base his argument that when doctors medically foreshorten a life, they are doing so actively?
3. To what does Doyal attribute the cancellation of his speech on euthanasia?

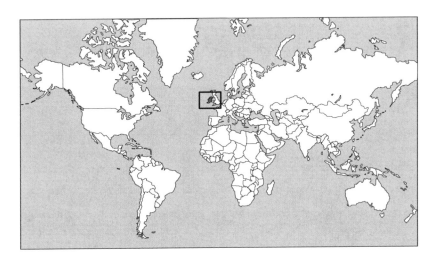

Because of the refusal to let me speak in Ireland [in 2009], my arguments for the legalisation of euthanasia have unfortunately been lost in the noise surrounding the non-event. . . .

This has been especially evident in the press and on the Internet where I have been subjected to intense abuse based on erroneous beliefs about my position.

For example, I have never argued, as many have claimed, that involuntary euthanasia should be legalised or that money could be saved by the state through killing vulnerable or elderly people. Nor have I argued that the law should be broken, but rather that it should be changed.

Many of the public debates following the cancellation of my talk compounded misunderstanding rather than clarifying the reality of current medical practice, and exploring some of the confusion in its legal and moral underpinnings. This saddens me.

My views on euthanasia are based only on the search for moral coherence and on compassion for those whom I have been accused of wishing to harm. I hope very much that the important arguments outlined below can now be debated openly in Ireland.

Doctors Already Help Shorten Lives

The main aim of my talk was to demonstrate that many doctors are already involved in shortening the lives of patients, in Ireland and elsewhere. This occurs when decisions are made either not to provide or to withdraw life-sustaining treatments to patients who are severely brain damaged and have no actual or potential quality of life. Such individuals—often neonates or adults in intensive care—may still have the potential for suffering but are not in a position to communicate this to those caring for them. Under these circumstances, it will often be decided that continued life-sustaining treatment is not in their best interests.

Doctors, nurses and family members may then make a decision to foreshorten the patient's life by not sustaining it medically, stopping the provision of ventilator support for example. How long the death of such a patient will then take depends on the type of treatment to be withdrawn and the patient's clinical condition. For some it may involve a lengthy period of suffering, for themselves and their families.

These actions are not carried out to save money or to rid society of "undesirables". Rather they are done because the lives of those concerned are deemed to be no longer worth living. Remember, the purpose of life-sustaining treatment is precisely that: to sustain life. If such treatment is deemed to be of no benefit to the patient, it must be because a prior decision has been made that life itself is of no benefit to them and hence life-sustaining treatment is not in their best interest. Indeed, a doctor who did not make such a decision would arguably be in violation of his duty of care. Under these circumstances, what kind of moral sense does it make to force patients to die slowly when they could do so quickly with compassion and care? Why allow any vulnerable patient to suffer a slow death when a quick and painless one could easily be provided were non-voluntary euthanasia to be legalised?

When doctors medically foreshorten life in this way they do so actively and not just passively. This is often denied and their actions are said to have nothing to do with euthanasia. It is argued that they are in fact doing nothing at all—other than "letting nature take its course" or "omitting" to act. Yet the idea that withdrawing ventilator support or other forms of life-sustaining treatment from a patient is not an action is absurd. Switches must be flipped, drips removed. Positive acts such as these that lead to patients dying take place regularly in Irish hospitals. These should not be denied but acknowledged and embraced as humanitarian interventions for some patients.

What kind of moral sense does it make to force patients to die slowly when they could do so quickly with compassion and care?

Justifying Medical Shortening of Life

So how are these actions justified in a society where euthanasia itself is so vehemently opposed by some sections of society?

One important argument used to square this apparent circle is that doctors who withdraw treatment can be deemed to be morally righteous if they do so with the aim of relieving the patient's suffering rather than taking away [his/her] life. It is claimed that the legalisation of euthanasia is wrong because it enables doctors to act with the transparent intention of killing.

This is also a weak argument. Remember that when a decision is made either not to provide or to withdraw life-sustaining treatment, there has already been a prior judgment that the patient's life is no longer worth living.

So why should the intent to bring about death after such a decision be morally worse than the intent to relieve suffering?

> ## The Terminology of Euthanasia in Ireland
>
> | Terminology | Definition |
> | --- | --- |
> | Voluntary Euthanasia | The action of a third party, which deliberately ends the life of an individual, with that individual's consent. |
> | Non-voluntary Euthanasia | Where the individual is unable to ask for euthanasia and another person makes the decision on his/her behalf, usually based on previously expressed wishes. |
> | Assisted Suicide | Where an individual takes his/her own life based on information, guidance and/or medication provided by a third party. |
> | Physician Assisted Suicide | Where a doctor provides the information, guidance and/or medication with which an individual can take his/her own life. |
>
> TAKEN FROM: The Irish Council for Bioethics, "Euthanasia: Your Body, Your Death, Your Choice?" 2010. www.bioethics.ie.

In circumstances where the palliative relief of suffering may be unachievable or unavailable, the intent to administer a quick and painless death should be seen as a more morally worthy goal.

The Interests of the Patient Should Prevail

If the parents and health care team of a 23-week-old severely damaged neonate agreed that life was of no further benefit to the baby, we would presumably be unimpressed by a senior consultant who said that he would not flip the switch because he had become unsure of his own intentions! The best interests of the child should prevail; not the subjective feelings of the doctor.

Doctors should be able to abide by their commitment to minimize suffering. For some patients, this will entail ending life quickly.

So much for the argument in support of the legalisation and regulation of non-voluntary euthanasia. If this argument is correct, the case for voluntary euthanasia directly follows. If doctors are enabled to make these decisions on behalf of severely brain damaged and incompetent patients, why should competent and suffering patients who are terminally ill not be allowed to make the same decisions for themselves?

Despite frequent claims to the contrary, there is no good evidence that the legalisation of euthanasia will lead to widespread and unjustified killing of patients. Contrary to what is often claimed, scholarly research has shown that this has not been the case in Holland for example.

At present, the potential suffering of vulnerable patients who might be frightened by the prospect of euthanasia—however well regulated—is given more weight than the actual suffering of competent and incompetent patients who in too many cases are ending their lives in pain and distress.

Despite frequent claims to the contrary, there is no good evidence that the legalisation of euthanasia will lead to widespread and unjustified killing of patients.

What kind of compassion—Christian or otherwise—is that? It seems to me that this exercise of arbitrary prejudice is a violation of even the simplest principles of moral equality, presumably on the grounds of religious beliefs which many of those thus deprived of the right to a quick and easy death may not themselves hold.

Whether or not readers agree with the preceding arguments, I hope that it is now clear that they would have served to promote an interesting debate in Cork [a city in Ireland]. I regret that dogmatism, apparently fuelled by religion, and lack of respect for free speech prevented this [speech]. Beware, it could happen again!

Australians Debate the Medical Ethics of Euthanasia

Wendy Zukerman

In the following viewpoint, Wendy Zukerman reports on legislation that would permit voluntary euthanasia under certain circumstances in some Australian states. She cites statistics demonstrating that most Australians favor voluntary euthanasia in some circumstances. However, studies also provide evidence that doctors are not in favor of such statutes. In addition, certain religious beliefs affect how lawmakers and the public view voluntary euthanasia. Consequently, the subject is the topic of heated debate across the Australian state legislatures. Zukerman is a science reporter who often writes for the Australian *newspaper.*

As you read, consider the following questions:

1. What percentage of Australians approve of a doctor providing a lethal dose to a suffering patient if the patient has no chance of recovery, according to a poll?

2. According to the viewpoint, what is the primary drug used in the Netherlands, Belgium, and Luxembourg during legalized euthanasia?

3. From what did Christian Rossiter eventually die, as Zukerman reports?

Wendy Zukerman, "States Debate Euthanasia," *The Australian*, November 7, 2009. Reproduced by permission of the author.

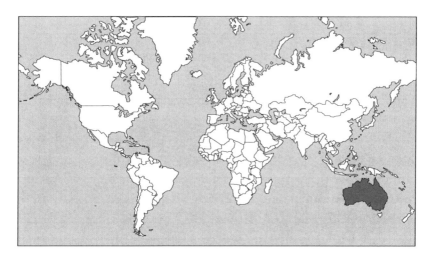

Christian Rossiter was quadriplegic, unable to move except to wriggle a finger and slightly shuffle his feet. He was fed with a tube in his stomach and could only talk through a tracheotomy, a hole in his neck. Rossiter wasn't mentally ill. Nor was he dying. If given food and water through the tube he could have lived for many years. But this wasn't what he wanted.

Rossiter described life trapped inside his crippled body as a living hell and wanted to die. In August [2009] the Supreme Court of Western Australia upheld Rossiter's right to refuse medical treatment. Chief Justice Wayne Martin authorised his carers to remove the feeding tube, allowing him to starve to death. "I am happy that I have won my right to die," Rossiter said after the decision was announced.

While this case was not about euthanasia—defined by the Australian Medical Association as a doctor actively providing lethal treatment to consenting patients—it was about a suffering individual's right to choose how he die.

Euthanasia Is Supported by Most Australians

Euthanasia isn't legal under Australian law but is supported by most Australians. Last week [in late 2009], for instance, a

Newspoll of 1201 Australians found 85 per cent approved of a doctor providing a lethal dose to a suffering patient with no chance of recovering, after the patient requested the dose.

Still, many state legislators don't agree. Just this week [November 2009] a bill to legalise euthanasia was voted down by the Tasmanian Parliament.

But in response to Rossiter's story, the Greens' [an Australian political party] Robin Chapple plans to introduce a voluntary euthanasia bill into WA [West Australia's legislature] within weeks, and there are moves afoot to reintroduce a bill in Victoria [a state in Australia] after next elections.

Meanwhile, South Australian independent MP [member of Parliament] Bob Such has introducted a similar bill into the lower house that's yet to have its second reading, but a bill introduced by his Greens counterpart in the upper house, Mark Parnell, last week narrowly passed its second reading and is scheduled for a third reading on November 18. However, the bill may not be read in the Lower House until after the SA [South Australia] elections next March.

"This bill is bringing into light that things are happening in the dark," says Parnell. According to him, each week four elderly Australians kill themselves by violent and undignified means.

Under the bill, SA doctors would be allowed to administer drugs to end the life of an eligible individual. "The person must be an adult in the terminal phase of a terminal illness or have an illness that results in permanent deprivation of consciousness or irreversibly impairs the person's quality of life so that life has become intolerable," explains Parnell.

His bill also would set up a regime whereby a patient seeking to die must be assessed by [his/her] doctor twice and get approval from a psychiatrist. Finally, the request would have to be sanctioned by a new voluntary euthanasia board comprised of medical and legal experts. "If the doctor [or board] believes the patient is acting under duress, which includes imagined duress like people thinking: 'I'm a burden to

Doctors and End of Life Care

A 2007 survey in Australia and six European nations questioned doctors whether they had
• ever withheld and/or withdrawn treatment taking into account the probability or certainty that this would hasten the end of the patient's life;
• never withheld and/or withdrawn treatment, but would be willing to do so under certain conditions;
• never withheld and/or withdrawn treatment and would never do so.

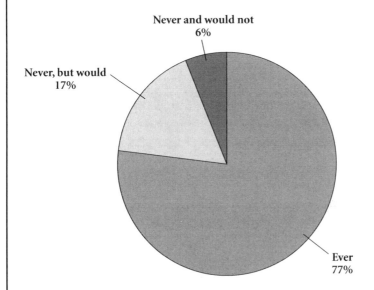

TAKEN FROM: Rurik Löfmark, et. al., "Physicians' Experience with End-of-Life Decision-Making: Survey in 6 European Countries and Australia," *BMC Medicine*, Vol. 6, No. 4, February 12, 2008. www.biomedcentral.com/1741-7015/6/4.

the family", the euthanasia request will not be granted," Parnell says. Once the board approves the application, the doctor can administer drugs to end life or prescribe them to a patient for self-administration.

Family First MLC [member of the Legislative Council] Dennis Hood, who voted against the bill, disagrees with the legislation's eligibility criteria.

"It's incredibly reckless to not even require that someone is terminally ill," Hood says. "They merely have to find their life intolerable, which is a subjective term. What is intolerable today may not be intolerable tomorrow due to changing circumstances or even medical advances."

While amendments will be made to the bill before its third and final reading, Hood says he still won't support it.

"I think it's impossible to legislate to ensure that no mistakes occur," he says. "And because a mistake when you talk about euthanasia is a fatal mistake there is no chance of making amends to the victim or their family."

Conversely, pro-euthanasia activist Philip Nitschke believes "it's an extremely cautious piece of legislation". After all, requiring individuals to apply to a government board before being granted approval "doesn't appeal to many people", he claims. [As of May 2010, none of the bills mentioned have been passed.]

Euthanasia Is Illegal

At present in Australia it's illegal for doctors to intentionally administer lethal treatment and there's no legal recognition of an individual's right to die. Patients do have the right [to] refuse medical treatment, as seen in Rossiter's case. But this is hardly a reassuring solution for people forced to starve or suffocate to death by refusing nutrition or oxygen.

Doctors may also legally administer drugs knowing they'll hasten a patient's death so long as the doctor intends only to relieve pain. However, there can be a fine line between unlawful and lawful administration of painkillers. "The fear of prosecution does inhibit doctors using pain medication as they should," says Rodney Syme, a medical practitioner for 45 years and vice president of Dying with Dignity Victoria. He adds: "Even in palliative care situations, patients can get inadequate pain control."

Several jurisdictions worldwide, including the Netherlands, Belgium and Luxembourg, have legalised euthanasia. According to Nitschke, the primary drug used in these countries is a barbiturate, Nembutal or pentobarbital. Known as the "green dream", it's used by vets to euthanise animals. It was once prescribed to people as a sleeping pill but was pulled off the Australian market in 1998.

Nitschke says: "Barbiturates are readily absorbed orally. They first affect the sleep centre and as more of the drug passes through the brain they depress respiratory centres. People go into a deeper and deeper sleep. To anyone watching you can't imagine anything more peaceful."

[In 2008] a survey of 1478 Australian doctors found 64 per cent would never prescribe or supply drugs with the explicit intention of hastening the end of life after receiving a request from a patient.

Doctors Do Not Support Euthanasia

Despite consistent public support for legalised euthanasia, the medical community doesn't agree. Last year, a survey of 1478 Australian doctors found 64 per cent would never prescribe or supply drugs with the explicit intention of hastening the end of life after receiving a request from a patient. The Australian Medical Association [AMA] policy reflects this opinion.

"It doesn't support euthanasia," says AMA president Andrew Pesce. "The AMA position is that doctors shouldn't administer treatment whose only intention is to end life." He adds despite the recent Newspoll, "there hasn't been enough discussion in the public for us to be certain about what society feels about this".

But Pesce says if such a discussion took place and clearly demonstrated support for euthanasia, that would guide the AMA's view.

Legal issues also affect the association's anti-euthanasia policy, he says. "The AMA would never have an official position to ask doctors to act in disregard of the law."

An important explanation for divergent views on euthanasia in the medical, legal and wider community is religion. A large Victorian-based study found one-third of doctors opposed to euthanasia derived their views from religious beliefs.

Religion Affects Attitudes Toward Euthanasia

This year Australian National University sociologist Joanna Sikora researched the relationship between religion and Australians' attitudes to euthanasia. She found a clear correlation between some religious beliefs and opposition to euthanasia.

Sikora says: "The ideology that the Catholic social doctrine has provided is commitment to the belief that life was not created by humans and cannot be taken away by humans."

Parnell believes these traditional ideas are changing: "The view that life must be kept going at all cost is being looked at differently when people see the suffering that that can lead to."

For instance, under present WA laws, Rossiter was given the right to die but he wasn't allowed a peaceful death.

While preparing to starve to death, a chest infection intervened. Rossiter refused antibiotics and died from the infection in September.

In the United Kingdom, Euthanasia Should Be Legal

Raymond Tallis

In the following viewpoint, writer/physician Raymond Tallis argues for the legalization of physician-assisted euthanasia. Although he previously opposed such legislation, Tallis reports that he changed his mind based on evidence demonstrating that even the best palliative care cannot always ensure pain-free death. In addition, Tallis notes, evidence from Oregon and the Netherlands proves that the rates of nonvoluntary euthanasia have gone down in places that have legalized assisted dying. Tallis concludes that the law denying help for terminally ill patients who want to die is cruel.

As you read, consider the following questions:

1. What is the name of the Oregon law that permits assisted suicide?
2. What European country had the highest level of trust between patient and doctor in a nine-country survey?
3. According to a study published in *Palliative Medicine* in 2009, what was the percentage of assisted deaths in the United Kingdom, despite the law banning euthanasia?

Raymond Tallis, "Why I Changed My Mind on Assisted Dying," *TimesOnline*, October 27, 2009. Reproduced by permission.

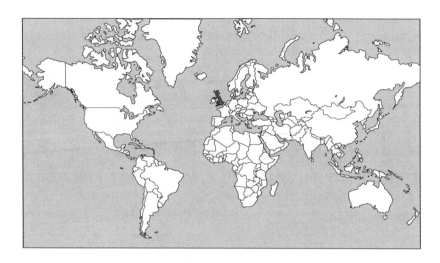

This week [October 2009] Debbie Purdy [a British activist who suffers from multiple sclerosis] and I will be arguing for the legalisation of physician-assisted dying at the Battle of Ideas in London. A few years ago I might have been on the other side of the argument.

When I was chairman of the Committee for Ethical Issues in Medicine at the Royal College of Physicians, we twice considered bills put forward by Lord [Joel] Joffe [a member of the British House of Lords] proposing to legalise the choice of physician-assisted dying for mentally competent people with terminal illness who were suffering unbearably at the end of their lives. On the first occasion, we decided to oppose the bill and on the second, because we were divided, we opted for neutrality.

The case for such a bill to me now seems clear. Unbearable suffering, prolonged by medical care, and inflicted on a dying patient who wishes to die, is unequivocally a bad thing. And respect for individual autonomy—the right to have one's choices supported by others, to determine one's own best interest, when one is of sound mind—is a sovereign principle. Nobody else's personal views should override this.

Evidence Supports Euthanasia

So where did my initial opposition come from? I was in thrall to numerous incorrect assumptions. But the evidence changed my mind.

Several of my assumptions related to palliative care. Wouldn't assisted dying be unnecessary if the best palliative care were universally available? This is not true and I should have acknowledged this from my experience as a doctor for more than 35 years, when I treated patients whose symptoms were uncontrolled even when they had first-rate palliative care. International experience also confirms that palliative care fails some patients. For the last ten years, assisted suicide has been legal in Oregon under the Death with Dignity Act. Oregon has among the best palliative care of all the states in America and yet nearly 90 per cent of those seeking assisted dying do so from within those services.

I was advised that the availability of assisted dying as an "easy" option would inhibit investment in palliative care. Again, international experience does not support this. In many countries, legalisation of voluntary euthanasia has been accompanied by increasing investment in palliative care services. In Oregon the proportion of people dying in hospice care has more than doubled since the Death with Dignity Act was introduced.

I also shared the worry that legalising assisted suicide would break down trust between doctor and patient. This is not borne out by the evidence. A survey of nine European countries put levels of trust in the Netherlands at the top. And this is not surprising: In countries with assisted dying, discussion of life care is open, transparent, honest and mature, not concealed beneath a cloud of ambiguity, as it is in the UK [United Kingdom]. And the knowledge that your doctor will not abandon the therapeutic alliance with you at your hour of greatest need will foster, not undermine, trust.

The British Support Assisted Suicide

According to a 2010 poll, 1,010 British residents responded overwhelmingly in favor of legally allowing a family member or friend to help a person who suffers from a painful, terminal illness to die.

A family member or friend should be able to legally assist a terminally ill person to die.

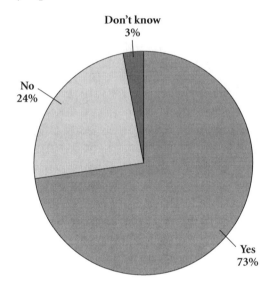

Don't know
3%

No
24%

Yes
73%

TAKEN FROM: ComRes for BBC Panorama, Assisted Suicide Survey, January 8–10, 2010.

I was also concerned that legalising assisted suicide would take us to the top of a slippery slope leading to the involuntary euthanasia of people who do not wish to die. In fact, to use the ethicist John Harris's phrase, if there is a slippery slope, legislation would apply crampons rather than skis.

Evidence from Oregon and the Netherlands

In Oregon, where assisted dying legislation is close to the Joffe proposal, the numbers and kinds of people being helped to die have not changed over a decade. The Dutch experience was to me decisive. Rates of nonvoluntary euthanasia (i.e., doctors actively ending patients' lives without having been asked by them to do so) decreased from 0.8 per cent of all deaths in 1991 (1,000 deaths) to 0.4 per cent in 2005 (550 deaths).

In the UK, a study published in *Palliative Medicine* this year [2009] found that more than 1 in 200 deaths were assisted, three-fifths of which were cases of ending life without explicit request. This means that a few thousand people each year receive assistance to die. The present clinical, ethical and legal fudge—in which ploys such as continuous sedation, and starvation and dehydration, are used to get round the prohibition on assisted dying—is unacceptable.

As a geriatrician, I was also worried that assisted dying would be offered to, or imposed upon, those who are most disempowered. A very detailed analysis of the data in Oregon has shown that there is an underrepresentation of those groups and an overrepresentation of comparatively well-off, middle-class white people—feisty characters who are used to getting their own way.

These were the facts that prompted me to change my mind. Even those who accepted these facts still opposed legislation on the grounds that only a small minority of dying people would seek assistance and an even smaller number would use the prescription. Wouldn't legislation prove a sledgehammer to crack a nut?

The ability of assisted dying would bring much comfort to many more sufferers than actually use it because it brings a sense of having some control.

The Present Law Is Cruel

Well, I happen to believe that even small numbers of people going through unbearable hell are important. The availability of assisted dying would bring much comfort to many more sufferers than actually use it because it brings a sense of having some control.

Death from dehydration and starvation in patients who have no means of securing an end to their suffering other than by refusing food and fluids, or botched suicides, reflect the unspeakable cruelty of the present law. To accede to someone's request for assisted dying under the circumstances envisaged in the Joffe bill is not to devalue human life, or devalue the life of a particular human being, or to collude in their devaluing their own life. It is to accept their valuation of a few remaining days or weeks of life that they do not wish to endure.

As a result of the courageous action of Debbie Purdy, supported by Dignity in Dying, those who assist their loved ones on grim pilgrimages to Switzerland may be confident that they will not face prosecution. But we have a legal vacuum. Legalisation of physician-assisted dying is needed urgently.

In the United Kingdom, Euthanasia Should Be Illegal

Melanie Phillips

In the following viewpoint, Melanie Phillips argues that it is "barbaric" to suggest that elderly people with dementia should be subjected to euthanasia in order to make life better for their caregivers. She asserts that active euthanasia (acting with the intention of ending the life of a patient who would not otherwise be dead) is murder. Further, she contends that there is a crucial moral distinction between giving a patient a drug that relieves pain but may also hasten his or her death, and giving a patient a drug with the intention of ending his or her life. Phillips is a columnist for the London Daily Mail.

As you read, consider the following questions:

1. Who is Baroness Mary Warnock and what does she believe regarding euthanasia, in Phillips's view?
2. What did the Law Lords' judgment in 1993 allow doctors to do?
3. According to Phillips, what do consequentialists think about human life?

Has there ever been anyone who has displayed more inhumanity towards her fellow human beings, and yet had more influence over British society, than the noble Baroness

Melanie Phillips, "So Now Our Intellectuals Think the Old and Frail Have a 'Duty to Die.' Truly, We Are on the Path to Barbarism," *Daily Mail* (London), September 22, 2008, p. 14. Copyright © 2008 Solo Syndication Limited. Reproduced by permission.

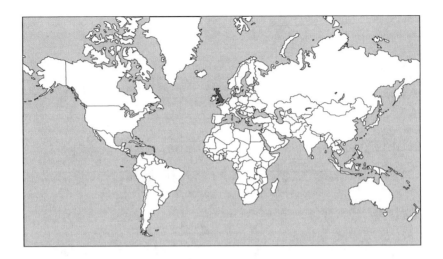

[Mary] Warnock [a British philosopher and writer]? In an article for a church magazine [in 2008], Lady Warnock has declared that elderly people with dementia are 'wasting' the lives of those who care for them, and have a duty to die in order to stop being a burden to others.

Sufferers and relatives should be helped through the provision of better treatments and improvements in care.

A Barbaric Point of View

This is a truly barbaric point of view. It regards other human beings as worthless and expendable simply because they can no longer care for [themselves.] On pitiless Planet Warnock, people are valued in proportion to their ability to lead an independent life. If they can't do so, they are to be written off as valueless—and even more nauseating, they are being told they actually have a duty to end their lives.

The elderly and chronically sick—indeed, anyone who constantly depends on others for care—often dread being a burden on their nearest and dearest. To be told that they must end this burden by finishing themselves off can only increase their guilt, despair and suffering.

On Planet Warnock, it seems that ties of family and kinship, acts of selfless love, the deep satisfaction from bringing comfort to those who are helpless or who are so poignantly leaving us—essential aspects of our common humanity—mean nothing at all.

Chilling to be sure, those who are forced to watch a spouse or close relative descend into dementia often suffer immeasurably from this tragic process. All the more reason, therefore, for protecting those who have lost their minds from any pressure from relatives to end their lives, and not—as Lady Warnock is doing—adding to that pressure still further.

Sufferers and relatives should be helped through the provision of better treatments and improvements in care. To say that the demented should instead end their lives shows a quite chilling absence of elementary human sympathy.

A Question of Method

And just how does she propose such people should bring this about? She is, after all, talking about people who have lost their minds. How can people who are mentally incapable possibly be expected to take such a decision? Does she mean they should take it before their minds have disintegrated—in which case, their quality of life will still be good and the pressure on relatives will be relatively light? Should their 'duty' to die perhaps kick in the very moment they receive the diagnosis of dementia? Or does she mean that all of us should sign living wills instructing doctors to end our lives if we should ever suffer from dementia in the future—without knowing whether we would be a burden on anyone at all, or indeed whether, if such a disease did strike us down, we would still rather like to continue to live, thanks very much? One gets the feeling that such practicalities don't matter much to Lady Warnock. What drives her is simply the belief that lives which she considers to be worthless should be ended. Down this particular road, of course, lie the historic spectres of eugenics, the concentration camp and the gulag [Soviet political prison].

Tempting though it may be, it would be a mistake to treat this elderly philosopher as an eccentric who can be safely ignored.

Lady Warnock is a key figure in the development of medical ethics in this country, from research on embryos to the debates over euthanasia.

Sliding Down a Slippery Slope

Although the days when governments called upon her to serve on such committees of the great and the good may be over, her thinking provides graphic evidence of the slippery slope down which we are sliding at terrifying speed.

What she originally presented as the 'right to die', for example, soon mutated into the 'duty to die'. The claim that euthanasia would benefit sick people by ending their pain is thus revealed as a fraud. The real point is to benefit the sick person's relatives, in whose interests the patient must be expected to forfeit life itself.

For the 'right to die', therefore, read instead 'no right to live'.

The impulse to end lives considered to be worthless is sliding from cases involving people in an irreversible coma to people who still have their senses, but have lost the power of rational thought.

The watershed was the Law Lords' judgment in 1993 that allowed doctors to withdraw feeding and hydration from Anthony Bland, the Hillsborough victim who had been left in a persistent vegetative state.

Subsequently, the Mental Capacity Act, which came into force last year [2007] in the face of huge disquiet and after a

A Duty to Die?

Already the public debate and the popularity of assisted dying is ratcheting up the anxiety of the dying. The relationship of trust with medical staff—crucial to effective care—is being compromised. It's not hard to see how seamlessly the prevalent fear of being a burden among the elderly could morph into feeling it was their duty to die.

Madeleine Bunting,
"Gilderdale's Trial Was Horrific but Necessary
to Retain a Vital Principle," Guardian,
February 8, 2010. www.guardian.co.uk.

fudged amendment by the Lords, allowed the withdrawal of food and water from patients who are unable to give their consent.

Both Parliament and the courts insist that these developments merely 'allow' patients to die and do not legalise intentional killing.

A Crucial Distinction

But this is simply slippery semantics. These measures do not 'allow' patients to die for the simple reason that they are not already dying.

They are actions taken with the intention of ending the lives of people who otherwise would not be dead.

And that, in plain language, is killing.

The distinction is absolutely crucial. Yet it is one that Lady Warnock refuses to acknowledge.

She has said that the difference between killing and 'allowing to die' is a 'wholly bogus distinction'.

It is a view she carried into practice when she watched her incurably ill husband, Geoffrey, accept the help of a family doctor to take lethal doses of morphine in order to end his life.

This is because Lady Warnock's thinking follows the 'consequentialist' doctrine which looks at the result of an action, regardless of its motive. Hence, she sees no distinction between a drug administered to alleviate a dying patient's suffering that ends up hastening that person's death, and a drug deliberately given to bring about death.

But intention is the essence of morality.

It means the difference between murder and manslaughter; between an attack and an accident; between killing and allowing someone to die.

Consequentialists similarly think there is no intrinsic value in a human life; the only value lies in the quality of the life that is being lived. That's why Lady Warnock thinks that if people have lost their faculties, they should forfeit their existence to benefit others whose lives are—in her eyes—worth more.

A terrifying, amoral landscape is opening up before us . . . where the weakest are being steadily sacrificed for the benefit of the strong.

This is indeed the path to barbarism. But Lady Warnock is by no means alone in holding these views. They are mainstream among our secular, anti-religious elites—and alarmingly, nowhere more so than in the medical profession.

The Royal College of Obstetricians and Gynaecologists, for example, said two years ago that 'active euthanasia' should be considered to spare parents the emotional and financial burden of bringing up seriously disabled newborn babies. These doctors were advocating killing newborn infants for the presumed benefit of others.

A terrifying, amoral landscape is opening up before us, brought into being by the philosophy embodied by Lady Warnock—the garlanded intellectual, whose epitaph will be a dehumanised society where the weakest are being steadily sacrificed for the benefit of the strong. This is the way civilisation dies.

Canadian Ethicists Debate the Definition of Death

Stuart Laidlaw

Canadian faith and ethics reporter Stuart Laidlaw investigates in the following viewpoint the ethical debate surrounding determination of death. Technology can keep people alive when their own brains and/or hearts stop working, Laidlaw notes, so the historic means of determining death no longer are always relevant. To organ transplantation, this is crucial, Laidlaw contends, since organs must be harvested quickly. Cardiac death cannot be declared for several minutes after the heart has stopped beating, potentially damaging the value of the heart for transplant. Additionally, the Catholic Church is questioning brain death, according to Laidlaw, adding to the controversy.

As you read, consider the following questions:

1. What three cases caused the determination of death to become a matter of public debate, according to Laidlaw?
2. Who is Kaylee Vitelli and what happened to her?
3. In Catholic hospitals, according to Laidlaw, how long after cardiac death are doctors waiting before they remove a patient's heart for transplant?

Stuart Laidlaw, "Dead When the Doctor Says You Are: Ethicists Wrestle with the Changing Nature—and Timing—of Death," *TheStar.com*, April 15, 2009. Reproduced by permission of Torstar Syndication Services.

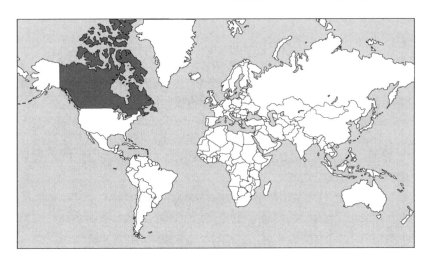

D ead is dead, except when it's not.

"Death used to be a little more self-evident," says Kerry Bowman, a medical ethicist specializing in end-of-life issues at the University of Toronto's Joint Centre for Bioethics.

"Today, you're dead when the doctor says you are."

A Top Ethical Issue

Deciding when somebody is dead or about to die is quickly emerging as one of the top ethical issues in medicine today as technology makes it increasingly possible to keep people alive who would otherwise have died not so long ago.

"The technology has far outstripped the ethics," says Tim Falconer, author of *That Good Night: Ethicists, Euthanasia and End-of-Life Care*. "Feeding tubes and ventilators weren't designed to keep people alive for 15 years, but that's what they're being used for."

As well, says Bowman, with organ transplants more common, deciding the precise moment of death has become vital, since under the "dead donor rule" organs can only be harvested once the donor has died. And the sooner after death that happens, the healthier the organs will be.

Such issues become matters of public debate when cases arise like that of Terri Schiavo in the United States or Italy's Eluana Englaro, in which families fight publicly with medical officials over whether to maintain life support. A generation ago, the case of Karen Ann Quinlan of New Jersey captured headlines when her parents fought to let her die in her persistent vegetative state. They won the right to remove her respirator in 1976, but she lived in a coma, breathing on her own, until 1985.

And just last week [in April 2009] in Toronto, the debate began again with the case of 2-month-old Kaylee Vitelli at the Hospital for Sick Children, whose parents were told she could not live without a respirator and wanted to donate her heart to another baby at the hospital.

With organ transplants more common, deciding the precise moment of death has become vital, since under the "dead donor rule" organs can only be harvested once the donor has died.

But when the respirator was removed to make way for the transplant, Kaylee kept breathing—forcing all those involved to question their assumptions about her seeming impending death. Yesterday she was continuing to breathe with oxygen assistance.

"This little girl just wasn't ready to die," says Moira Mc-Queen, director of the Canadian Catholic Bioethics Institute. McQueen worries about a blurring of the line between dying and dead, saying we sometimes treat people as already dead once they are deemed terminal—a notion Kaylee challenged with her survival.

Brain Death vs. Cardiac Death

Organ donations most often take place after brain death, a concept articulated 40 years ago at Harvard University and meaning the irreversible end of all brain activity.

In a brain dead patient, the brain no longer tells the body to keep living, so machines do that, instead.

Brain dead soon came to replace the historic understanding of death—the heart stopping. After all, a stopped heart no longer seemed relevant when machines could keep a heart beating indefinitely.

However, the increased popularity of donation after cardiac death, or the harvesting of organs from patients whose hearts have been allowed to stop beating, has once again got the medical community looking at how to define death according to the functions of the heart.

Like Kaylee, such donors are often on life support because of an illness or disability that requires them to be permanently hooked up to machines. Removing those machines means death by cardiac arrest.

The Ethical Questions of Heart Transplants

While doctors have long harvested organs such as kidneys and livers from such patients, taking a heart is relatively new. That's because cardiac death requires the person to be dead for several minutes before the heart can be taken out. In that time, the heart is damaged.

How long to wait is a matter of heated debate. One recent study recommends taking out the heart 75 seconds after it stops. The standard in most jurisdictions, including Canada, is five minutes. Catholic hospitals, McQueen says, are increasingly moving to 10 minutes "to be doubly sure" the patient is dead.

But in a series of articles last summer, the prestigious *New England Journal of Medicine* questioned whether heart transplants after cardiac death are inherently unethical, since the criteria for taking the heart out of the donor is that the patient's death be irreversible.

The problem, the *Journal* said, is that the donated heart is soon restarted in another body—which means it could probably have been restarted in its original body, as well, raising the question of whether the donor was, in fact, irreversibly dead.

"If a heart is restarted, the person from whom it was taken cannot have been dead according to cardiac criteria," wrote Robert [M.] Veatch, professor of medical ethics at the Kennedy Institute of Ethics at Georgetown University.

In such a case, Veatch writes, death was caused by the donation of the heart, not its stopping.

Such quandaries make donation after cardiac death very problematic for many people.

Determining Death Is a Complicated Issue

In recent months, even the long-held acceptance of brain death has been called into question, particularly in the Catholic Church.

Last summer, a front-page column in the Vatican newspaper *L'Osservatore Romano* questioned whether brain death violates traditional Catholic teaching by equating human life with brain activity only. It pointed to the case of a brain dead pregnant woman who was able to give birth to her child.

McQueen says the column did not shake Vatican support for the brain death definition, adding she draws a distinction between "being alive" and "being *kept* alive" by machines.

When cases like that of Kaylee come along and capture the public's imagination, Falconer says, it unleashes a debate about death and dying. "This is a discussion we need to have."

Periodical and Internet Sources Bibliography

The following articles have been selected to supplement the diverse views presented in this chapter.

Lucy Bannerman	"Baroness Warnock: Euthanasia Abroad Would Mean a 'Two-Tier Death Service,'" *Times* (UK), October 4, 2008.
Tom Blackwell	"Ethicist Seeks Law to Say When Dead Is Truly Dead; Cites Growing Use of Organs from Cardiac Victims," *National Post* (Canada), July 17, 2009.
Cathy Lynn Grossman	"Matters of Life and Death: Hospital Ethics Panels Help Families Make Hard Choices," *USA Today*, October 8, 2009.
Dominic Lawson	"The Door to Euthanasia Stays Shut, as It Must," *Sunday Times* (UK), February 28, 2010.
Stephanie Nano	"Doctors Debate When to Declare Organ Donors Dead," *USA Today*, August 16, 2008.
Pulse	"Should GPs Play a Role in Assisting a Patient's Death?" November 11, 2009.
Susan Sachs	"How Dead Is Dead? Revival of 'Dead' Man Being Prepared for Organ Donation Sparks French Ethics Debate," *Straits Times* (Singapore), June 15, 2008.
Arthur Schafer	"The Great Canadian Euthanasia Debate," *Globe and Mail* (Canada), November 5, 2009.
Rob Stein	"Heart Pump Creates Life-Death Ethical Dilemmas," *Washington Post*, April 24, 2008.
Douglas Todd	"A Moral Question of How to Die," *Vancouver Sun* (Canada), January 30, 2010.

GLOBALVIEWPOINTS

| Medical Ethics and
| Organ Transplantation

Worldwide, Doctors Consider Global Organ Trafficking Unethical

Debra A. Budiani-Saberi and Francis L. Delmonico

In the following viewpoint, Debra A. Budiani-Saberi and Francis L. Delmonico report on their study of the buying and selling of organs on the global market in countries such as Pakistan, India, the Philippines, Egypt, Slovenia, and elsewhere. In addition, they surveyed commercial living donors throughout the world to judge the outcome of their kidney donations. They conclude that organ trafficking exploits the poor and vulnerable of the world who have nothing else to sell but their vital organs. The authors list the ethical practices that must be put in place worldwide. Budiani-Saberi is a bioethicist at the University of Pennsylvania, and Delmonico is a professor of surgery at Harvard Medical School.

As you read, consider the following questions:

1. What reason does the viewpoint give for opposing organ trafficking?
2. What percentage of kidney transplants around the world does Yosuke Shimazono estimate occur via the organ trade?

Debra A. Budiani-Saberi and Francis L. Delmonico, "Organ Trafficking and Transplant Tourism: A Commentary on Global Realities," *American Journal of Transplantation*, vol. 8, January 2008, pp. 925–929. *American Journal of Transplantation* by American Society of Transplant Surgeons. Copyright © 2008 Basil Blackwell Ltd. Reproduced by permission of BLACKWELL PUBLISHING in the format Journal via Copyright Clearance Center.

3. What four goals do the authors cite from the Kuwait Statement that would lead toward more ethical organ transplantation?

Organ trafficking brings little regard for the well-being of the donor. Who cares for the donor in the early period following transplantation or in the long term, especially if complications arise? This [viewpoint] will describe the organ trafficking known to the authors by their visits to many countries on behalf of The Transplantation Society (TTS) and the World Health Organization [WHO] and by the field research and advocacy work with commercial living donors (CLDs) of the Coalition for Organ-Failure Solutions (COFS). It introduces alternative approaches that must be addressed by each country to combat organ trafficking.

An Ethical Issue for Transplant Clinicians

The buying and selling of organs in the global markets has become an ethical issue for transplant clinicians everywhere in the world. Even physicians who would have no part in the organ trade now bear a responsibility for the medical care of those recipients who return to their home countries having undergone organ transplantation from an unknown vendor. These recipients arrive at physician offices in widespread locations such as Tel Aviv, Toronto and Trinidad. Some patients return home with inadequate reports of operative events and unknown risks of donor-transmitted infection (such as hepatitis or tuberculosis) or a donor-transmitted malignancy. The source of their allografts [transplanted organs] is mainly from the poor and vulnerable in the developing world. These vendors or commercial living donors resort to an organ sale because they have virtually no other means to provide support for themselves or their families. Selling kidneys may be a consideration of 'autonomy' in academic debate but it is not the coercive reality of experience when a kidney sale is a desperate alternative available to the poor. . . .

Definition of Organ Trafficking and Transplant Tourism

The discourse on the market of organs has used various terms to describe the commercialism at the core of organ trafficking. The seller of a kidney is not only the donor source of an organ but a vendor whose motivation is monetary gain. The following definition of organ trafficking is derived from the United Nations [Office on Drugs and Crime]. Organ trafficking entails the recruitment, transport, transfer, harboring or receipt of persons, by means of the threat or use of force or other forms of coercion, of abduction, of fraud, of deception, of the abuse of power, of a position of vulnerability, of the giving or receiving of payments or benefits to achieve the consent of a person having control over another person, for the purpose of exploitation by the removal of organs, tissues or cells for transplantation. The reason to oppose organ trafficking is the global injustice of using a vulnerable segment of a country or population as a source of organs (vulnerable defined by social status, ethnicity, gender or age).

> *Vendors or commercial living donors resort to an organ sale because they have virtually no other means to provide support for themselves or their families.*

This definition of organ trafficking captures the various exploitative measures used in the processes of soliciting a donor in a commercial transplant. Exploitation is the threat or use of force or other forms of coercion, abduction, fraud, deception, abuse of power or position of vulnerability. The commercial transaction is a central aspect of organ trafficking; the organ becomes a commodity and financial considerations become the priority for the involved parties instead of the health and well-being of the donors and recipients.

Transplant tourism has become a connotation for organ trafficking. The United Network for Organ Sharing (UNOS), recently defined transplant tourism as 'the purchase of a transplant organ abroad that includes access to an organ while bypassing laws, rules, or processes of any or all countries involved'. However, not all medical tourism that entails the travel of transplant recipients or donors across national borders is organ trafficking. Transplant tourism may be legal and appropriate. Examples include, when travel of a related donor and recipient pair is from countries without transplant services to countries where organ transplantation is performed or if an individual travels across borders to donate or receive a transplant via a relative. Any official regulated bilateral or multi-lateral organ sharing program is not considered transplant tourism if it is based on a reciprocated organ sharing program among jurisdictions. . . .

The Extent of Organ Trafficking

Countries that have facilitated organ trafficking such as Pakistan and the Philippines do not release precise data (not surprisingly) regarding the numbers of foreign patients that travel to these countries for transplants. In the Philippines, a quota of foreign nationals was intended but there has been no report of data to indicate that such a stipulation has been fulfilled. Despite its clandestine nature and the difficulties in obtaining national data, the extent of organ trafficking has become evident by our visits to many countries around the world and by reports prepared for presentation at the WHO.

According to data from the Sindh Institute of Urology and Transplantation (SIUT), at least 2000 kidney transplants have been performed in Pakistan to transplant tourists. The widespread dimension of these practices becomes particularly evident, when a highly regarded nephrologist in Port of Spain Trinidad reports that a series of 80 patients had gone from Trinidad to Pakistan to buy organs.

In the Philippines, a February 2007 newspaper account of the number of kidney sales reveals over 3000 have been performed. The WHO held a regional consultation in Manila to call attention to its objection to the rampant commercialism. The Cebu Province of the Philippines is now reported to be seeking transplant tourists to increase Philippine commercial transplants.

It is estimated by Egyptian transplant professionals that we both have visited, that Egypt performs at least 500 kidney transplants annually. A majority of these transplants are performed from CLDs.

[Investigative journalist] Scott Carney reports that transplant tourists have undergone kidney transplantation from tsunami victims in Chennai, India.

At the WHO regional consultation in Slovenia, the representative from Moldova reported the request of Israeli physicians to set up a transplantation practice in that country. The request was denied but there is no current penalty being imposed upon the insurance companies that are systematically enabling these transplants to occur outside of Israel. As many as 20 patients from Israel may currently undergo kidney transplantation in the Philippines each month. The consequence for Israel is that the expertise in performing organ transplantation within Israel may be lost. Hopefully, the pending legislation in the Knesset [Israeli legislature] on organ transplantation will address this issue.

A Sampling of Trafficking Data

At the Second Global Consultation on [Critical Issues in] Human Transplantation at the WHO headquarters in Geneva in 2007, [Oxford University anthropologist Yosuke] Shimazono also assembled a sampling of the trafficking by an analysis of databases such as LexisNexis, MEDLINE and PubMed academic journal articles, and Google searches that included media sources, transplant tourism websites, renal and transplant registries and reports from health authorities. Shimazono estimated that 5–10% of kidney transplants performed annually around the globe are currently via organ trade. The credibility of this estimate is given by the following data: at least 100 nationals from countries such as Saudi Arabia (700 in 2005), Taiwan (450 in 2005), Malaysia (131 in 2004) and South Korea (124 in the first 8 months of 2004) went abroad annually for a commercial kidney transplant. At least 20 nationals from other countries such as Australia, Japan, Oman, Morocco, India, Canada and the United States traveled as transplant tourists for trafficked organs. But the more striking observation comes from the revelation of data in a visit to China in the summer of 2007. In 2006, 11000 transplants were performed in China from executed prisoners. There were 8000 kidney transplants, 3000 liver transplants and approximately 200 heart transplants. The 8000 kidney transplants alone in China in 2006 would account for at least 10% of the total number of annual organ transplants done in programs of organ trafficking. It should be noted that since China's recently adopted human transplantation act that bans commercialism was adopted in May 2007, China has reduced the number of transplants to foreign patients by 50% in 2007. Nevertheless, the reduction in Chinese activity has presumably been supplanted by an increase in Philippine organ trafficking.

[Dr. Robert M.] Merion [and his colleagues] have reported the initial US experience that includes some patients whose transplants were not obtained from CLDs. One hundred nineteen US citizens and resident aliens from 55 transplant centers in 26 states were recorded as having received kidney transplants in 18 foreign countries after a median of 1.5 years (range 21 days to 8.5 years) on the US waiting list. HRSA [Health Resources and Services Administration] officials who collaborated with Dr. Merion are now aware of this practice and should be following it closely. There is a public hazard for patients to return from out of country with potential transmissible infection such as avian flu, tuberculosis, Schistosomiasis [a parasitic disease], acute hepatitis and/or HIV [human immunodeficiency virus] infection.

Recipients of commercial transplants abroad should not be denied the provision of follow-up care; yet there is no justification to condone illegal transplants outside United States if the purchase of a kidney (that could result in Medicare benefits to be received for immunosuppressive medications) is illegal within the borders of the United States. The legislation that is being considered by the Knesset in Israel would prohibit the insurance reimbursement of transplant costs for Israelis that undergo a purchased organ transplant in countries where the buying and selling of organs is illegal. . . .

[Commercial living donors in Pakistan] who sold a kidney to repay a debt . . . reported no economic improvement in their lives, as they were either still in debt or were unable to achieve their objective in selling the kidney.

The Consequence to the Vendors

What then of this emerging worldwide population of live kidney vendors? In Pakistan, the SIUT group has carefully detailed a sample cohort of (239) vendors in a follow-up—the outcomes all very troubling. The majority of these [were] CLDs (93%) who sold a kidney to repay a debt and (85%) reported no economic improvement in their lives, as they were either still in debt or were unable to achieve their objective in selling the kidney. The disturbing report by the SIUT group becomes not only an accounting of the Pakistani experience but an indictment of the international transplant community because it overlooks the plight of the donor whose interests are just as valid as the recipients.

Egypt is one of the few countries that prohibits organ donation from deceased donors. In the absence of an entity to govern allocation or standards for transplants, the market has become the distribution mechanism. Egypt is also one of the countries in which COFS has conducted extensive field research and long-term outreach service programs for victims of the organ trade. In-depth longitudinal interviews conducted by [COFS director Debra] Budiani[-Saberi] reveal that 78% of the CLDs reported a deterioration in their health condition. This is likely a result of factors such as insufficient donor medical screening for a donation, preexisting compromised health conditions of CLD groups and that the majority of employed CLDs reported working in labor-intensive jobs. A kidney sale does not solve the most frequently given reason for being a CLD, 81% spent the money within 5 months of the nephrectomy, mostly to pay off financial debts rather than investing in quality of life enhancements. CLDs are not eager to reveal their identity; 91% expressed social isolation about their donation and 85% were unwilling to be known publicly as an organ vendor. Ninety-four percent regretted their donation.

The studies in Pakistan and Egypt are consistent with findings in India, Iran and the Philippines that revealed deterioration in the health condition of the CLDs. A long-term financial disadvantage is evident following nephrectomy from a compromised ability to generate a prior income level. The common experience also entails a social rejection and regret about their commercial donation. These reports are consistent with the COFS experience in the CLD interviews; a cash payment does not solve the destitution of the vendor. . . .

Ethical Protocols Must Be Established

Transplants conducted in countries with loose or no legal frameworks such as that of Pakistan, the Philippines and Egypt accommodate the organ market and the transplant tourists that drive the demand. Engaging governments to play a central role in establishing laws on transplants and for the Minis-

Definitions in the Organ Market

Organ trafficking is the recruitment, transport, transfer, harboring or receipt of living or deceased persons or their organs by means of the threat or use of force or other forms of coercion, of abduction, of fraud, of deception, of the abuse of power or of a position of vulnerability, or of the giving to, or the receiving by, a third party of payments or benefits to achieve the transfer of control over the potential donor, for the purpose of exploitation by the removal of organs for transplantation.

Transplant commercialism is a policy or practice in which an organ is treated as a commodity, including by being bought or sold or used for material gain.

Travel for transplantation is the movement of organs, donors, recipients, or transplant professionals across jurisdictional borders for transplantation purposes. Travel for transplantation becomes *transplant tourism* if it involves organ trafficking and/or transplant commercialism or if the resources (organs, professionals, and transplant centers) devoted to providing transplants to patients from outside a country undermine the country's ability to provide transplant services for its own population.

"Declaration of Istanbul on Organ Trafficking and Transplant Tourism," Clinical Journal of the American Society of Nephrology, *vol. 3, 2008, p. 1228.*

try of Health to carry out oversight of transplant practices is an essential component to improve the global situation of organ trafficking/transplant tourism. . . .

Each country should establish a system of deceased organ donation. At a WHO regional consultation on developing organ donation from deceased donors, held in Kuwait City last year [2007], transplant professionals from Bahrain, Iran, Jordan, Kuwait, Lebanon, Libya, Morocco, Oman, Pakistan, Qatar, Saudi Arabia, Sudan, Syria, Tunisia, United Arab Emirates and Yemen supported the development and expansion of organ and tissue donation from deceased donors. They opposed commercialism and transplant tourism, including brokerage and medical professionals seeking monetary profit as a result of the vendor sale or coerced donation of an organ or tissue. The Kuwait Statement was crafted with an eye towards the following goals:

- Each country must develop a legal framework and national self-sufficiency in organ donation and transplantation;

- Each country must have a transparency of transplantation practice that is accountable to the health authorities and whose authority is derived from national legislation;

- Countries in which the buying and selling of organs is outlawed must not permit their citizens to travel to destination countries and return for insured health care in the client country; and

- Insurance companies should not support illegal practices as they are doing preferentially in some countries.

This list is not exhaustive of approaches that can improve the care of the live donor consistent with the recommendations of the Amsterdam Forum [on the Care of the Live Kidney Donor]. Proposals are now being made to address additional measures to improve donor safety. These aims of the Kuwait Statement are also elaborated in the drafted and updated WHO guiding principles. This document is a product of the recommendations from global experts who participated in several WHO regional consultations hosted in diverse locations such as Khartoum, Manila, Slovenia and Geneva. The WHO guiding principles emphasize that 'organs, tissues and cells should only be donated freely and without monetary reward. The sale of organs, tissues and cells for transplantation by living persons, or by the next of kin for deceased persons, should be banned. However, the prohibition of sale or purchase of cells, tissue and organs does not affect reimbursing for reasonable expenses incurred by the donor, including loss of income, or the payment of other expenses relating to the costs of recovering, processing, preserving and supplying human cells, tissues or organs for transplantation'.

The international transplant community must deliver a concerted message that organ markets that exploit the poor and vulnerable are not acceptable.

Drug Companies Should Be Made Accountable

Additionally, corporations such as pharmaceutical companies involved in transplants and insurance companies should also be made accountable for their engagement in processes, which prioritize profit generation at the disregard of social justice. TTS has addressed each of the major pharmaceutical representatives involved in transplantation to solicit support for its global mission to combat organ trafficking. Further, various insurance programs (both public and private) in countries as diverse in resources as the US, Israel, Yemen and Saudi Arabia, should not encourage patients to seek a transplant abroad without regard to the source of the organ. These countries cannot overlook the plight of the donor and condemn organ sales within the country and condone the commercialism outside its borders. There is precedent in international law to prohibit illegal practices irrespective of national borders, for example, in the bribery of public officials.

The international transplant community must deliver a concerted message that organ markets that exploit the poor and vulnerable are not acceptable, but programs must be developed alternatively that assure donor safety and provide social benefits that address donor needs. These needs are the legitimate consequences of living organ donation and must be addressed in each country with Ministry of Health oversight, authorized by national legislation and guided by the World Health Assembly [the decision-making body of WHO] resolution.

In Scotland, a System of Presumed Consent Would Solve the Organ Shortage

Anne Johnstone

In the following viewpoint, Anne Johnstone asserts that longer life expectancy in the richer nations of the world has led to a shortage of kidneys for transplant in these nations. As a result, she argues, poor people around the world are selling their kidneys in the global organ market. She opposes the sale of organs on moral grounds and because it undermines a system of selfless donation where individuals volunteer to help others. She contends that if Scotland initiated a system of presumed consent, whereby consent to donate organs is presumed unless a person opts out, many more organs would be available for transplant and would alleviate the organ shortage, thereby saving lives. Johnstone is a columnist for Herald Scotland.

As you read, consider the following questions:

1. How much money does Johnstone assert the transplant tourism industry is worth?
2. What did anthropology professor Nancy Scheper-Hughes find out about those who sell their kidneys?
3. What was the Alder Hey scandal, according to the author?

Anne Johnstone, "Danger of the Disgusting Trade in Human Organs," *Herald Scotland*, April 24, 2008. Copyright © 2008 Johnston Publishing Ltd. Reproduced by permission.

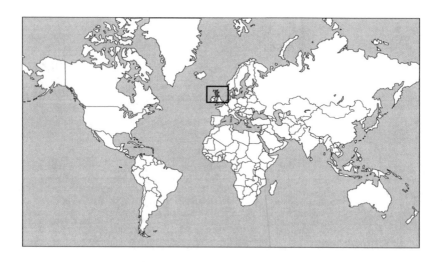

How much would you pay for a kidney? It's a question most of us wouldn't care to answer and hope we'll never need to ask. We assume that if our kidneys fail, either someone else's death would give us the gift of life or that someone genetically or emotionally related to us would bravely come to the rescue.

The inconvenient truth is that across the world the gap between the numbers waiting for transplants and the supply of organs is getting bigger. In the rich world, rising living standards and medical advances are extending life expectancies, producing an ever-expanding population of sick, elderly people in need of further repair. While the illnesses of old age cause more cases of kidney failure, advances in transplant surgery make spare-part surgery almost as routine as changing the oil filter on the family jalopy. So where are all these extra organs to come from?

The Market Economy of Organs

As usual, global market economics has come up with a neat answer, at least it has for kidneys, because in his infinite wisdom God has given us two, though strictly speaking we need only one. There are a billion people in the world trying to live on 50p [about $.75 USD] a day and billions more up to their ears in debt. Sooner or later it was inevitable that unscrupulous entrepreneurs operating globally would work out that a lot of money could be made by linking the desperately ill with the desperately poor.

A conference in Istanbul this week [April 2008] is looking at "transplant tourism", a growing industry worth an estimated £1bn [$1.5 billion USD] a year. At least 10,000 people annually are being paid to donate kidneys. Organ trafficking probably accounts for about 10% of transplants worldwide, according to the World Health Organization. Here's a hypothetical scenario: a poor young Brazilian labourer, mired in debt, is befriended by an agent who offers him £3000 [$4,500 USD] if he will sell a kidney. He agrees and travels to South Africa, where he waits until the patient, a rich elderly American, arrives at a nearby private clinic. The Brazilian signs forms, including one that says he's related to the recipient, though they have never met. Then a top surgeon performs the transplant. The American pays £30,000 [$45,000 USD]. The deal is brokered by an international organ trader.

The commodification of body parts is wrong and . . . organ trafficking simply exploits the desperation of both buyer and seller and encourages what could be called a modern form of cannibalism.

There is a school of thought that maintains this is a perfectly legitimate transaction, a simple example of the economics of supply and demand. The impoverished donor has his debts wiped out. The rich recipient has a new lease of life. Win, win. People sell their labour, sex, sperm, ova. What's so special about kidneys? In certain cases—soldiers on active service and surrogate mothers, for instance—the entire body is essentially a commodity, so why can't a kidney be one, too?

Some use the same argument for legalising organ trafficking that is applied to abortions: that those involved are more at risk when it is underground and legalisation hands to the state control over standards, payments, aftercare and the like. In one scenario, the state would buy kidneys and allocate them on whatever basis it choses.

The Commodification of Body Parts

There's so much wrong with these arguments that it's hard to know where to begin. For a start, it is often not a win-win situation at all. Anthropology professor Nancy Scheper-Hughes, director of the pressure group Organs Watch, has found that within five years of selling a kidney, sellers are just as poor as before, often because they are unable to work for a time and lose their jobs. (The surgery is more invasive and debilitating than many are led to believe.) Some sellers are so desperate for money that they will agree to sell for as little as £250 [$375 USD]. And some are promised a small fortune, then cheated by the broker.

Also, you don't need to be either religious or superstitious to believe that the commodification of body parts is wrong and that organ trafficking simply exploits the desperation of both buyer and seller and encourages what could be called a modern form of cannibalism. Japanese sociologist Tsuyoshi Awaya describes it like this: "We are now eyeing each others' bodies greedily, as a potential source of detachable spare parts with which to extend our lives."

Of course, we should be concerned that even in a country like Scotland, there's a huge gap in health and life expectancy between rich and poor. Even more fundamentally immoral, surely, is a trade where organs move only one way: from the poor to the rich. Predominantly, it is also from black, brown and yellow people to white ones and from women to men. Will the sellers ever get transplants if they need them? Unlikely. And we can't leave it to hospitals to decide if a donor is

---

2009 Snapshot of Organ Donation, Scotland and the United Kingdom

• Percentage of people who say they support organ donation: 90%

• Percentage of people who are registered with the National Health Service as organ donors: 27%

• Percentage of Scots who are registered organ donors: 32%

• Percentage of Londoners who are registered organ donors: 22%

• Number of people on the active waiting list for an organ transplant: 7,986

• Number of organ donations carried out in the [United Kingdom] from April 1, 2008 to March 31, 2009: 3,513

• Number of people on the waiting list in Scotland: 778

• Number of organ transplants in Scotland in 2008: 210

National Health Service Blood and Transplant (NHSBT), 2009.
www.nhsbt.nhs.uk.

---

acting under duress or because of extreme need because donors would lie out of desperation.

Organ Trafficking Threatens Legitimate Donations

Perhaps the worst aspect of all this is the way organ trafficking threatens legitimate donation by disrupting what is known as "the gift relationship". This is where members of society voluntarily make selfless gestures for the good of society as a whole, without accruing any direct benefit. Carrying an organ donor card is one of the most obvious examples. This week Euro MPs [members of Parliament] called for an EU [European Union]-wide donor card scheme to tackle the increasing shortage of organs. One of their fears is that the mounting commercial trade in kidneys, especially from the poor East European accession states, could undermine legitimate donation in countries where it is well established. Once a monetary value is put on a kidney, people would be less willing to consider donating them freely.

A UN [United Nations] conference in Vienna last month named Australia, Canada, Israel, Japan, Oman, Saudi Arabia and the US as "major organ-importing countries". The big exporters of kidneys from live donors include Brazil and India, where 43-year-old Dr Amit Kumar allegedly made millions by persuading hundreds of the poor to give up their kidneys, which were sold to rich Greek, American and British patients. He was arrested in February after a police raid. And though it's illegal to buy or sell human organs in China, an undercover BBC investigation last year suggested that death row prisoners (officially around 1700 a year but believed to be many more) "volunteered" to give their organs as a "present to society". Some end up on the international market.

Globally, a properly regulated system of presumed consent would save the lives of thousands who die, often in terrible pain, while waiting for transplants.

Presumed Consent Will Save Lives

All this should bring into sharp focus the debate in Britain over presumed consent [a system by which it is presumed a person has consented to donate organs upon death unless he or she has specifically stated otherwise]. The last time the issue came before MPs, very soon after the Alder Hey scandal (about dead children's body parts being stored without consent), understandably it received short shrift. Now the climate is more favourable and both [British prime minister] Gordon Brown and Nicola Sturgeon [deputy first minister of Scotland] seem receptive.

Of course, the very idea provoked a charge of the right-wing ideological cavalry, ranting about "state-sponsored body snatchers" and spreading scare stories about people losing their eyes and livers before they were "really dead". Yet globally, a properly regulated system of presumed consent would save the lives of thousands who die, often in terrible pain, while waiting for transplants. And it would undermine the cruel exploitation of poor people in the name of a disgusting form of medical apartheid.

By the way, anyone who wants my kidneys ("one careless owner"), after I've finished with them, is more than welcome.

China Takes Steps Against Organ Trafficking

Debarati Mukherjee

Debarati Mukherjee has been an editor for the Telegraph *and a writer for* Deutsche Welle. *In the following viewpoint, the author writes that China began its first voluntary organ donation program in 2009. The country suffers from a severe shortage of organs for transplantation, partially because of the traditional Chinese belief that the body should be whole to enable reincarnation into another body without physical disabilities. Consequently, China has relied heavily on organ donations from executed prisoners. Voluntary donation by condemned prisoners is very suspect, and it is believed that many people are condemned for the sake of obtaining their organs. There is also an illegal trade in human organs. The author reports that China is now instituting a voluntary organ donation program, and experts believe that this will make it more difficult for foreign transplant tourists to come to China to buy organs.*

As you read, consider the following questions:

1. According to the author, how many Chinese prisoners does Amnesty International estimate were executed in 2008?

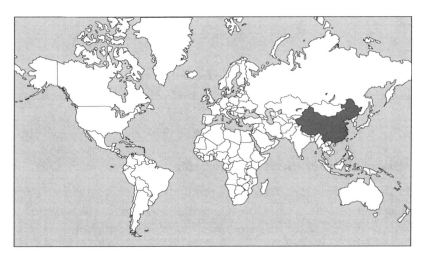

2. Who is Dr. Francis Delmonico, and what does he say about written consent from condemned prisoners to donate their organs?
3. What is a health hazard associated with using organs from executed prisoners?

Nearly two-thirds of China's transplanted organs come from executed prisoners, the Chinese state media reported last week. In a bid to curb the illegal trade in human organs, the government has now launched an official organ donation scheme. It hopes this will encourage people to become voluntary donors.

The Chinese Vice Minister of Health, Huang Jiefu, announced that about 65 percent of the organs transplanted in Chinese hospitals come from convicts put to death for various crimes. China does not release any figures on the number of executions, but Amnesty International estimates that over 1,700 prisoners were executed in 2008, making China the world leader as far as the implementation of the death penalty is concerned.

Dr. Wenyi Wang is from the Washington-based rights group Doctors Against Forced Organ Harvesting, who graduated from a Chinese medical school and saw the way organs are removed from the executed prisoners, explains:

> The surgeon who is the chief of the residence goes to the executive prisoner's site where they execute the people by gunshot. Then they immediately transfer the prisoners into the room and extract the organs.

Prisoners Denied Basic Rights

Some Chinese officials however claim that the people condemned to die give written consent that they are willing to allow their organs to be donated. Dr. Francis Delmonico, Advisory for Human Transplantation, of World Health Organization argues:

> Not for a moment do I believe that this person is voluntarily giving. Here is a human reality that executions are now being fuelled by the need for human organs.

The Chinese traditionally believe that their body should be complete when they die so that it can be reincarnated for their next life without any physical disabilities. This makes organ donation among ordinary Chinese very much a taboo subject, even today. So, China still relies heavily on organs taken from executed prisoners. Critics say that a lot of young people are being sentenced to death for what people in the West would regard as relatively minor offenses, just to keep the supply of organs moving. Dr. Wenyi Wang explains:

> The person I first met in dealing with executed prisoners, when I was an intern in surgery, was very young, 18 years old and healthy. Basically his crime was that he had raped a woman who happened to be the daughter of the governor of our hometown. So they gave a phone call to the public security bureau and in three days, he was given the death sentence without any trial. In China the executed prisoners are considered to be an enemy of the country and have no rights. The government can do whatever it wants.

China Hosts Many Transplant Tourists

Organ transplantation is an established lifesaving procedure. Globalization of medical and surgical technology has increased the capacity for countries worldwide to perform organ transplantation. Unfortunately, dramatic geographic variation in the availability of organs for transplantation and a parallel discrepancy in financial resources for health care have increasingly led desperate patients to transplant tourism—traveling abroad to purchase donor organs and undergo organ transplantation.

In 2005, the World Health Organization (WHO) reported the transplantation of 66000 kidneys, 21000 livers, and 6000 hearts, with approximately 10% of these procedures occurring via transplant tourism. Leading destination countries for transplant tourism include China, India, the Philippines, and Pakistan. Globally, the number of organ transplant procedures in China is surpassed only by the US. According to the WHO, in 2005 China had 348 transplant centers, which performed 8204 kidney and 3493 liver transplantations. Although policy actions by China's Ministry of Health aimed at curbing transplant tourism to China have been reported, their impact is unclear.

Scott W. Biggins et al.,
"Transplant Tourism to China:
The Impact on Domestic Patient-Care Decisions,"
Clinical Transplantation, vol. 23, 2009, p.831.

Health Hazards

There are a lot of health hazards associated with taking organs from executed prisoners. Dr. Francis Delmonico explains:

The person that's being executed could have tuberculosis, hepatitis or other transmissible diseases that go by their being in the environment of the prison. One of the hazards of obtaining an organ from someone that's being executed is to not know what transmissible disease might come along with the organ.

But with the government's new scheme for the donation of organs, experts believe the situation will improve and that it will become more difficult for foreigners to come to China from rich countries in order to get a transplant. They also argue that international action should be taken to put an end to the illegal practice of transplant tourism.

In Hong Kong, Volunteer Organ Donations Cause Ethical Dilemmas

Ella Lee

In the following viewpoint, South China Morning Post *reporter Ella Lee writes on a new trend in Hong Kong, strangers volunteering to donate a portion of their livers to someone who needs it. Because the procedure puts a healthy person at risk, surgeons face an ethical dilemma, according to Lee. Donors must go through a lengthy process of gaining approval from the Human Organ Transplant Board and undergoing a psychological examination. Surgeons also want to set up protection for people who do not want to donate portions of their livers to family members, since it would not be ethical for them to be pressured.*

As you read, consider the following questions:

1. According to the viewpoint, how many cadaveric liver donations took place in Hong Kong in 2008?
2. How much of his or her liver will a healthy living donor have removed as a donation, as Lee describes?
3. What is the difference between a directed and non-directed donation?

Ella Lee, "Weighing Gifts of Life: A Burden for Doctors; Strangers' Offers of Liver Transplants for Hong King Patients Prompt an Ethical Debate Among Surgeons," *South China Morning Post*, July 23, 2009, p. 12. Reproduced by permission.

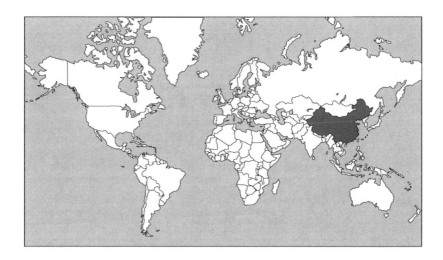

Wh en liver transplant surgeon Lo Chung-mau checked his e-mails a few months ago [in 2009], one message caught his eye. He could hardly believe what he was seeing: a young Pakistani wanted to donate a portion of his liver to anyone in Hong Kong who might need it.

Professor Lo, who is head of the University of Hong Kong liver transplant team at Queen Mary Hospital, said such a "good Samaritan act" raised more questions than answers.

Currently, more than 100 patients are awaiting the gift of life in the form of a liver transplant.

"This e-mail was a surprise to us," Professor Lo said. "We could not find a very convincing reason why this man wanted to travel a long way, to Hong Kong, to donate [part of] his liver. Perhaps this person does not exist."

After an exchange of e-mails, the transplant team asked to meet the man in person. But they never heard from him again.

A Growing Trend

The incident is part of a new and growing trend of people coming forward to donate to complete strangers in Hong Kong.

For the first time in Hong Kong, two people recently donated part of their livers to try to save patients they had never met. The donors, who responded to media appeals, gave to a 19-year-old woman and a 34-year-old mother, both suffering from acute liver failure.

Liver donations from the dead have reached a record high this year, with 31 cadaveric livers given in the first six months, compared with 29 in the whole of 2008.

But many patients still need living donors. Some families have made high-profile appeals in the media, which have raised public awareness and compassion.

For the first time in Hong Kong, two people recently donated part of their livers to try to save patients they had never met.

Professor Lo admitted that his team did not feel totally comfortable with this new trend.

"Organ donation from a stranger has become a challenge to us. We take a very cautious attitude towards this because we will be putting a perfectly healthy person at risk.

"First, we have to rule out any organ trading.

"Second, we have to make sure that a donor fully understands the risks he or she is facing."

Professor Lo said the team had been busy dealing with the flood of calls after each widely reported appeal.

"We explained to the callers in detail what the possible risk would be. A donor has to stay in hospital for at least a week and cannot work for six weeks. A big surgical scar will be left on the abdomen for life. Most of the people who called us withdrew after hearing such information. The whole process used up a lot of our manpower and resources."

The team also needs to assess a potential donor's mental state carefully. In one case, of a woman who contacted the team to donate part of her liver to a patient she did not know, doctors tracking her medical records found that she had a history of suicide attempts. Her offer was rejected on the grounds that she was mentally unstable.

For a typical adult recipient, a healthy living donor has 55 per cent of the liver removed. It will regenerate to function 100 per cent within four to six weeks, and will reach full size soon afterwards. The transplanted portion will reach full function and the appropriate size in the recipient as well, although it will take longer than for the donor.

Volunteer Donations Save Lives

When the family of 19-year-old Tiffany Law Man-ting appealed for help after she lapsed into a coma, suffering acute liver failure, five strangers contacted the transplant team. However, none went any further after learning about the risks involved in the operation.

Then 37-year-old Kenny Chan Kai-yiu—a devout Christian—appeared. Kelvin Ng Kwok-chai, the transplant team's consultant surgeon, interviewed him and was impressed by his determination. "He told us that God sent him here," Dr Ng said. "His mother is also a Christian and she fully supported him." The operation was carried out on September 25. Both Mr Chan and Ms Law have made a good recovery.

Mr Chan said: "I know a bit about liver transplants and I decided to give [part of] my liver to her. It was a magical feeling, it was like a calling from God to ask me to help this girl."

In the case of the 34-year-old, Flora Kwok Wing-mui, she suffered acute liver failure three weeks after giving birth to her son.

Her story hit the headlines and drew public attention.

A woman in her 30s—complete stranger—answered the call after reading the media reports. The transplant was carried out on December 4. The anonymous donor declined media interviews and did not even want to meet the patient.

Dr Ng said: "The donor said she only wanted to help the mother, she was so determined. She told us that she had prepared for the worst."

Directed vs. Non-Directed Donations

He said these two cases were classed as "directed" donations, meaning that the donors specified who the recipients would be.

The Pakistani case was the first "non-directed" donation that the team had come cross.

"We told him that organ trading is illegal in Hong Kong," Professor Lo said. "He stressed that he just wanted to donate [part of] his liver for free.

"We wanted to meet him but we do not hear from him any more."

Transplant surgeons have to be very careful in dealing with offers from living people unrelated to the patient, especially strangers.

First, an organ donation requires approval by the Human Organ Transplant Board, to rule out the possibility of organ trading.

Then doctors need to explain in detail the risks of the operation, which could kill the donor.

A clinical psychologist, the last gatekeeper, examines a prospective donor's mental state and his or her understanding of any adverse consequences of the operation.

"On the one hand, we have to be ethical and cautious; on the other hand, we have to do our best to save lives," Professor Lo said. "If we take any wrong step, the public will lose trust in us and the transplant programme we have established for years will collapse."

Medical Ethics and Organ Donations

Organ donations by strangers have also led to changes in health care policy and rethinks of medical ethics.

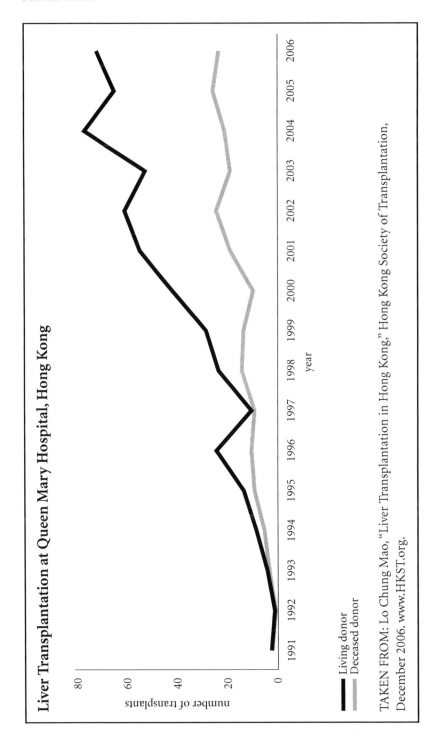

Liver Transplantation at Queen Mary Hospital, Hong Kong

number of transplants

Living donor
Deceased donor

year

TAKEN FROM: Lo Chung Mao, "Liver Transplantation in Hong Kong," Hong Kong Society of Transplantation, December 2006. www.HKST.org.

For example, the case in which a woman donated part of her liver to Ms Kwok has led to changes in the Hospital Authority's charging policy.

In the past, organ donors, usually close family members, had to pay all medical costs. Yet it appeared insensitive to ask payment from a stranger risking her life to help.

Organ donations by strangers have also led to changes in health care policy and rethinks of medical ethics.

"That donor did not expect a reward. She just found it unreasonable to pay the hospital bill. This case reminded us that something should be changed," Professor Lo said.

Alerted to the situation, Secretary for Food and Health York Chow Yat-ngok ordered a one-year waiver of medical fees for organ donors.

Since February, the Hospital Authority has waived all medical fees—including for hospital stays, medical investigations and pre-transplant counselling—for living organ donors for a year.

An authority spokesman said earlier: "It does not mean we encourage organ donations from living donors. We always promote organ donation from deceased patients."

Hong Kong Does Not Compensate Organ Donors

But Hong Kong is conservative when it comes to compensation for organ donors. While donors in the United States, Britain and Singapore are allowed under law to receive money, those in Hong Kong are not.

Professor Lo said Hong Kong doctors have reservations about such a compensation or award system. "In Canada, organ donors can get one-year income compensation. We don't encourage that practice, but we agreed that we should cover donors' medical bills."

He also revealed that some people are unwilling to donate part of their liver to family members, but instead prefer to make an appeal to the public. Based on advice from clinical psychologists, the team has recently agreed that doctors should make up "medical excuses" to protect these "unwilling" members.

"No person should be pressed to donate organs. If someone does not want to give [part of] a liver to a family member, we should protect him and make up a medical excuse," Professor Lo said.

"Public awareness towards organ donation is improving. Now we have cases where the families of the deceased have called us to offer to donate organs.

"But the supply will never be able to meet all the demand."

The European Union Opposes the Sale of Human Organs

Arthur Caplan et al.

In the following viewpoint, medical ethicist Arthur Caplan and his colleagues delineate the ethical framework for organ donations in the European Union (EU). The EU views the trade in human organs in the same ethical light as it views slavery, and it definitively prohibits the sale of organs. Organ donations must be voluntary. At the same time, steps must be taken to increase the number of organs available for transplantation. In addition, Caplan and his colleagues argue that presumed consent is ethical; that is, it is presumed that a deceased person wants to be a donor unless he or she has specified otherwise.

As you read, consider the following questions:

1. On what four key values is the existing European bio-ethical framework for obtaining tissues and organs based?

2. What are some of the steps taken by countries to increase the supply of organs in the authors' view?

3. As the viewpoint asserts, in what countries have laws establishing presumed consent been enacted?

Arthur Caplan et al., "Bioethics—the Ethical Framework for Organ and Tissue Procurement," in *Trafficking in Organs, Tissues and Cells and Trafficking in Human Beings for the Purpose of the Removal of Organs*, Joint Council of Europe/United Nations Study, Directorate General of Human Rights and Legal Affairs, Council of Europe, 2009, pp. 30–32. Copyright © 2009 Council of Europe. Reproduced by permission.

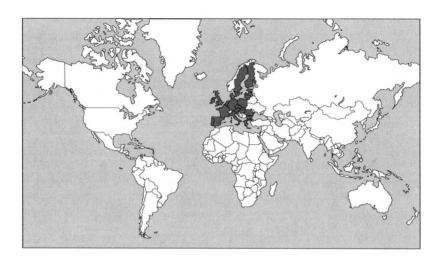

To close the gap between demand and supply of organs for transplantation, all manner of ideas are being floated on how to encourage people to give more organs when they die, optimise performance in the process of donation, enable more people to act as living donors and even find new sources of organs and tissues by rethinking organ procurement and the definition of who can be a deceased donor. . . . In order for policy makers to consider the merit of new options for encouraging people to donate OTC [organs, tissues, and cells] it is necessary fully to understand the bioethical framework that has guided organ and tissue donation in nearly every part of the world since its inception in the 1950s.

It is also necessary to think hard about the most effective and fair way of distributing scarce organs, including who on the waiting lists should receive transplants first. Fairness is a crucial element in determining the supply of donated organs and tissues. If the public does not believe the allocation of organs and tissues is fair, they will be far less willing to donate their organs or tissues upon their deaths or as living donors. Trust and altruism require fairness as a basis for organ and tissue donation.

The Bioethical Framework

The existing bioethical framework for obtaining organs and tissues is based on four key values—respect for individuals, autonomy, consent and altruism. The notion that organs or tissues can be removed for the purposes of transplantation, whether the individual concerned is alive or dead, without voluntary consent is one that has not been accepted except in highly unusual circumstances (i.e., unclaimed bodies at morgues in some countries). Individuals are recognised as having an interest in controlling their bodies in life and upon death. They are to be treated with dignity and not merely used to serve the health needs of others. So even though someone might well benefit from obtaining my liver or receiving bone marrow from my body, these organs and tissues ought not to be removed from me without my permission. To do so is to commit an assault upon a living person or to desecrate the body of a newly deceased person. Part of the notion of treating individuals with dignity is that they have control over what is done with their own bodies and their parts.

Another core element of the existing bioethical framework is that the body and its parts must not be made the subject of trade. The prohibition of slavery and of trafficking in persons for prostitution is based upon the ethical principle that human beings ought not to be bought and sold as objects, and transplantation has incorporated this view in the prohibition of trading in body parts for profit. In part, this is a bioethical view that rests upon the fundamental dignity of individuals. In part, it is a principle that reflects the huge dangers that would loom for human health and welfare if trade for profit in human body parts from the dead or the living were permitted. Altruism is the bioethical foundation as reflected in the use of the term "donation" for obtaining organs in a manner consistent with human dignity.

Donations Must Be Voluntary

In order to obtain organs and tissues from the living, there is agreement that, from an ethical standpoint, it is necessary to have a legally competent individual who is fully informed and can make a voluntary, uncoerced choice about donation. In cases where organs and tissues are sought from the deceased, the notion of voluntary consent has been extended in many countries to the recognition of donor cards or, for those not wishing to donate, the recording of objections in computer-based registries. While various policies about who is responsible for giving consent exist throughout the world, from a bioethical perspective, it is voluntary, informed consent that is crucial in making organ and tissue procurement ethical.

A core element of the existing bioethical framework is that the body and its parts must not be made the subject of trade.

Proposals to increase the supply of organs must be weighed up very carefully against this existing bioethical framework which has long been effective in protecting the interests of prospective donors. Changes in the relevant values might well alienate the public who have grown used to the existing bioethical framework, major religious groups who have long supported it or health care workers, the majority of whom firmly believe that the current bioethical framework is the right one for governing organ, tissue and cell procurement for transplantation purposes.

A number of steps have been taken over the years in many countries to try to increase the supply of organs. An early measure was to pass laws permitting the use of organ donor cards that enabled families to consent to donating a deceased relative's organs.

Some countries began requiring hospitals to ask all patients' families about organ and tissue donation upon death.

Presumed Consent in Europe and Around the World

Presumed consent is a system of organ donation that presumes that a deceased person gives consent for his or her organs being used for transplantation unless he or she has specifically indicated before death that he or she does not want to be a donor.

The following countries have enacted laws establishing presumed consent in organ donation:

Austria	Sweden
Spain	Switzerland
Portugal	Latvia
Italy	Czech Republic
Belgium	Slovak Republic
Bulgaria	Hungary
France	Slovenia
Luxembourg	Poland
Norway	Greece
Denmark	Singapore
Finland	

Compiled by editor.

Most recently, some countries now require hospitals to honour a patient's donor card even when a family member opposes donation.

While these policies have been effective, the gap in supply has continued to increase. Some people now therefore argue for a shift away from reliance on voluntary altruism in organ donation towards either a paid market or presumed consent.

Organ Markets

Two basic strategies have been proposed to provide incentives for people to sell their organs upon their deaths. One strategy is simply to permit organ sales by allowing individuals to broker contracts while alive with persons interested in buying at prices mutually agreed upon by both parties. At least in an underground sense, markets already exist on the Internet between potential live donors and people in need of organs.

The other strategy is a "regulated" market in which the government would act as the purchaser of organs—setting a fixed price and enforcing conditions of sale. Iran appears to have such a market in operation, although data on how it is specifically organised and how well it functions raise important ethical questions about the approach. In 1998, with a transplantation programme based on related living donors which was unable to cope with the demand for kidney transplantation within the country, a model of unrelated living donation, involving payments but controlled by the government, was developed in Iran. It is the government itself which remunerates the "voluntary" donors and provides them with one year medical insurance and with social recognition for the act of donation. The model has been shown to attain its objectives: Iran is the only country in the world with no waiting list for kidney transplantation, the system produces excellent post-transplant outcomes, and it has avoided the problem of transplant tourism by prohibiting transplantation to foreigners with organs from local donors. The supporters of this controlled organ trade state that it is the most suitable model in the particular context of the country, which might not be understandable from a Western perspective. However, Iranians have themselves openly recognised the limitations of this system, including the common additional remuneration usually paid by the recipient to the unrelated living donor.

Ethical Violations

Both proposals have drawn heated ethical criticism. One criticism is that only the poor and desperate will want to sell their body parts. If you need money, you might sell your kidney to try and feed your family or to pay back a debt. This may be a "rational" decision, but that does not make it a matter of free, voluntary choice. Watching your child go hungry when you have no job and a wealthy person waves a wad of money in your face is not exactly a scenario that inspires confidence in the "choice" made by those with few options but to sell body parts. Talk of individual rights and autonomy is hollow if those with no options must "choose" to sell their organs to purchase life's basic necessities. Choice requires information, options and some degree of freedom, as well as the ability to reason about risks without being blinded by the prospect of short-term gain.

Selling organs, even in a tightly regulated market, violates the existing bioethical framework of respect for individuals since the sale is clearly being driven by profit.

It is hard to imagine many people in wealthy countries being eager to sell their organs either while alive or upon their death. In fact, even if compensation is relatively high, few will agree to sell. That has been the experience with markets in human eggs for research purposes and with paid surrogacy in the United States—prices have escalated, but there are still relatively few sellers.

Selling organs, even in a tightly regulated market, violates the existing bioethical framework of respect for individuals since the sale is clearly being driven by profit. In the case of living persons, it also violates the ethics of medicine itself. The core ethical norm of the medical profession is the principle, "Do no harm." The only way that removing an organ from someone seems morally defensible is if the donor chooses to undergo the harm of surgery solely to make money.

The creation of a market in body parts puts medicine in the position of removing body parts from people solely to abet those people's interest in securing compensation as well as to let middlemen profit.

Is this a role that the health professions can ethically countenance? In a market—even a regulated one—doctors and nurses still would be using their skills to help living people harm themselves solely for money. In a deceased market, they would risk making families and patients uncertain about the degree to which appropriate care was being offered and continued and whether a person might be worth more 'dead than alive'. The resulting distrust and loss of professional standards is a high price to pay for gambling on the hope that a market might secure more organs and tissues for those in need.

Presumed Consent Is Ethical

There is another option for increasing organ supply that has been tried in countries such as Spain, Italy, Austria, Belgium and Singapore. These countries have passed laws establishing presumed consent. Under this system, the presumption is that a deceased person wishes to be an organ donor upon [his or her] death—basically an ethical default reflecting the desirability of donation. People who do not wish to be organ donors have to say so while alive by carrying a card indicating their objection or by registering their objection in a computerised registry or both. They may also tell their loved ones and rely on them to object should procurement present itself as an option.

What is important about this strategy from a bioethical perspective is that it is completely consistent with the existing bioethical framework governing organ and tissue procurement.

Respect for individuals and voluntary, altruistic consent remains the moral foundation for making organs available. The main ethical objection to presumed consent is fear of mistakes in the event of consent being presumed when, in fact, either the individual had failed to indicate [his or her] objection or the record of [his or her] objection had been lost.

Periodical and Internet Sources Bibliography

The following articles have been selected to supplement the diverse views presented in this chapter.

Guardian (UK)	"Organ Transplants: Relative Ethics," April 21, 2010.
Rina Jimenez-David	"At Large: Beyond the Urban Legend," *Philippine Daily Inquirer* (Philippines), July 24, 2009.
Brian Kates and William Sherman	"Rogue Kidney Brokers Resell Organs from Poorest Nations on Black Market," *Daily News* (New York), July 25, 2009.
Jeremy Laurance	"Change Law on Organ Donation, Doctors Say," *Independent* (UK), November 2, 2009.
Zubeida Mustafa	"Mr Shahbaz Sharif, Please Act," Dawn.com, June 18, 2009. www.dawn.com.
Martin O'Neill	"The Ethics of Organ Transplantation," *New Statesman*, January 16, 2008.
Brigid Schulte	"Faith Complicates a Young Mother's Life-or-Death Decision on Lung Transplant," *Washington Post*, February 17, 2010.
Ivan Semeniuk	"Interview: How We Tell Right from Wrong," *New Scientist*, March 3, 2007.
Yosuke Shimazono	"The State of the International Organ Trade: A Provisional Picture Based on Integration of Available Information," *Bulletin of the World Health Organization*, vol. 85, no. 12, December 2007.
Jerome Amir Singh	"Organ Transplantation Between HIV-Infected Patients," *Lancet*, February 6, 2010.
Mavis Toh	"The Village Organ Trader," *Straights Times* (Singapore), July 27, 2008.

GLOBAL VIEWPOINTS

CHAPTER 4

Ethics and
Medical Research

The World Medical Association Establishes Ethical Principles for Medical Research

The World Medical Association

In the following viewpoint, the World Medical Association (WMA) sets out the basic ethical principles that should underpin all medical research throughout the world. First and foremost, physicians and other medical professionals must protect the research subject. Although all medical research involves some risk, research subjects must be well informed, provide consent, and not be subjected to risks disproportionate to the potential benefit of the research. The WMA is an international organization of physicians dedicated to promoting the highest ethical standards for the medical research profession.

As you read, consider the following questions:

1. What is the primary purpose of medical research involving human subjects, according to the WMA?

2. What is the duty of physicians who participate in medical research, in the view of the WMA?

3. What are the ethical obligations of authors, editors, and publishers with regard to the publication of the results of research, according to the WMA?

The World Medical Association, "Declaration of Helsinki: Ethical Principles for Medical Research Involving Human Subjects," The World Medical Association, October 2008, pp. 1–5. Reproduced by permission.

The World Medical Association (WMA) has developed the Declaration of Helsinki as a statement of ethical principles for medical research involving human subjects, including research on identifiable human material and data. . . .

Although the Declaration is addressed primarily to physicians, the WMA encourages other participants in medical research involving human subjects to adopt these principles.

A Physician's Duty

It is the duty of the physician to promote and safeguard the health of patients, including those who are involved in medical research. The physician's knowledge and conscience are dedicated to the fulfillment of this duty.

The Declaration of Geneva [a declaration adopted by the WMA in 1948 affirming physician's dedication to humanity through medicine] of the WMA binds the physician with the words, "The health of my patient will be my first consideration," and the International Code of Medical Ethics [adopted by the WMA in 1949] declares that, "A physician shall act in the patient's best interest when providing medical care."

Medical progress is based on research that ultimately must include studies involving human subjects. Populations that are underrepresented in medical research should be provided appropriate access to participation in research.

Human Subjects in Medical Research

In medical research involving human subjects, the well-being of the individual research subject must take precedence over all other interests.

The primary purpose of medical research involving human subjects is to understand the causes, development and effects of diseases and improve preventive, diagnostic and therapeutic interventions (methods, procedures and treatments). Even the best current interventions must be evaluated continually through research for their safety, effectiveness, efficiency, accessibility and quality.

In medical practice and in medical research, most interventions involve risks and burdens.

In medical research involving human subjects, the well-being of the individual research subject must take precedence over all other interests.

Medical research is subject to ethical standards that promote respect for all human subjects and protect their health and rights. Some research populations are particularly vulnerable and need special protection. These include those who cannot give or refuse consent for themselves and those who may be vulnerable to coercion or undue influence.

Physicians should consider the ethical, legal and regulatory norms and standards for research involving human subjects in their own countries as well as applicable international norms and standards. No national or international ethical, legal or regulatory requirement should reduce or eliminate any of the protections for research subjects set forth in this Declaration.

Protecting Humans and Animals

It is the duty of physicians who participate in medical research to protect the life, health, dignity, integrity, right to self-determination, privacy, and confidentiality of personal information of research subjects.

Medical research involving human subjects must conform to generally accepted scientific principles, be based on a thorough knowledge of the scientific literature, other relevant sources of information, and adequate laboratory and, as appropriate, animal experimentation. The welfare of animals used for research must be respected.

Appropriate caution must be exercised in the conduct of medical research that may harm the environment.

The Research Protocol

The design and performance of each research study involving human subjects must be clearly described in a research protocol. The protocol should contain a statement of the ethical considerations involved and should indicate how the principles in this Declaration have been addressed. The protocol should include information regarding funding, sponsors, institutional affiliations, other potential conflicts of interest, incentives for subjects and provisions for treating and/or compensating subjects who are harmed as a consequence of participation in the research study. The protocol should describe arrangements for post-study access by study subjects to interventions identified as beneficial in the study or access to other appropriate care or benefits.

The research protocol must be submitted for consideration, comment, guidance and approval to a research ethics committee before the study begins. This committee must be independent of the researcher, the sponsor and any other undue influence. It must take into consideration the laws and regulations of the country or countries in which the research is to be performed as well as applicable international norms and standards but these must not be allowed to reduce or eliminate any of the protections for research subjects set forth in this Declaration. The committee must have the right to monitor ongoing studies. The researcher must provide monitoring information to the committee, especially information about any serious adverse events. No change to the protocol may be made without consideration and approval by the committee.

Medical research involving human subjects must be conducted only by individuals with the appropriate scientific training and qualifications. Research on patients or healthy volunteers requires the supervision of a competent and appropriately qualified physician or other health care professional. The responsibility for the protection of research subjects must always rest with the physician or other health care professional and never the research subjects, even though they have given consent.

The Risks and Benefits of Research

Medical research involving a disadvantaged or vulnerable population or community is only justified if the research is responsive to the health needs and priorities of this population or community and if there is a reasonable likelihood that this population or community stands to benefit from the results of the research.

Every medical research study involving human subjects must be preceded by careful assessment of predictable risks and burdens to the individuals and communities involved in the research in comparison with foreseeable benefits to them and to other individuals or communities affected by the condition under investigation.

Every clinical trial must be registered in a publicly accessible database before recruitment of the first subject.

Medical research involving human subjects may only be conducted if the importance of the objective outweighs the inherent risks and burdens to the research subjects.

Physicians may not participate in a research study involving human subjects unless they are confident that the risks involved have been adequately assessed and can be satisfactorily managed. Physicians must immediately stop a study when the risks are found to outweigh the potential benefits or when there is conclusive proof of positive and beneficial results.

Medical research involving human subjects may only be conducted if the importance of the objective outweighs the inherent risks and burdens to the research subjects.

The Origin of the Declaration of Helsinki

The DoH [Declaration of Helsinki] was first adopted at the 1964 WMA [World Medical Association] General Assembly in Helsinki. Its purpose was to provide guidance to physicians engaged in clinical research and its main focus was the responsibilities of researchers for the protection of research subjects. The advancement of medical science and the promotion of public health, although recognized as important objectives of medical research, were clearly subordinate to the well-being of individual research subjects. . . .

The DoH, like its well-known predecessor, the Nuremberg Code [a code of research ethics concerning human experimentation, adopted in 1947], was intended to prevent mistreatment of research subjects such as had been practised by Nazi physicians. In the absence of external constraints like legal frameworks and research ethics committees, it placed the responsibility to protect research subjects on medical researchers, who at that time were mostly physicians.

John R. Williams,
"The Declaration of Helsinki and Public Health,"
Bulletin of the World Health Organization,
vol. 86, August 2008, p. 650.

Research Subjects Must Be Well Informed

Participation by competent individuals as subjects in medical research must be voluntary. Although it may be appropriate to consult family members or community leaders, no competent individual may be enrolled in a research study unless he or she freely agrees.

Every precaution must be taken to protect the privacy of research subjects and the confidentiality of their personal information and to minimize the impact of the study on their physical, mental and social integrity.

In medical research involving competent human subjects, each potential subject must be adequately informed of the aims, methods, sources of funding, any possible conflicts of interest, institutional affiliations of the researcher, the anticipated benefits and potential risks of the study and the discomfort it may entail, and any other relevant aspects of the study. The potential subject must be informed of the right to refuse to participate in the study or to withdraw consent to participate at any time without reprisal. Special attention should be given to the specific information needs of individual potential subjects as well as to the methods used to deliver the information. After ensuring that the potential subject has understood the information, the physician or another appropriately qualified individual must then seek the potential subject's freely given informed consent, preferably in writing. If the consent cannot be expressed in writing, the non-written consent must be formally documented and witnessed.

For medical research using identifiable human material or data, physicians must normally seek consent for the collection, analysis, storage and/or reuse. There may be situations where consent would be impossible or impractical to obtain for such research or would pose a threat to the validity of the research. In such situations the research may be done only after consideration and approval of a research ethics committee.

Informed Consent

When seeking informed consent for participation in a research study the physician should be particularly cautious if the potential subject is in a dependent relationship with the physician or may consent under duress. In such situations the

informed consent should be sought by an appropriately qualified individual who is completely independent of this relationship.

For a potential research subject who is incompetent, the
physician must seek informed consent from the legally authorized representative. These individuals must not be included
in a research study that has no likelihood of benefit for them
unless it is intended to promote the health of the population
represented by the potential subject, the research cannot instead be performed with competent persons, and the research
entails only minimal risk and minimal burden.

When a potential research subject who is deemed incompetent is able to give assent to decisions about participation in
research, the physician must seek that assent in addition to
the consent of the legally authorized representative. The potential subject's dissent should be respected.

---

*The physician may combine medical research with medi-
cal care only to the extent that the research is justified by
its potential preventive, diagnostic or therapeutic value.*

Research involving subjects who are physically or mentally
incapable of giving consent, for example, unconscious patients, may be done only if the physical or mental condition
that prevents giving informed consent is a necessary charac-
teristic of the research population. In such circumstances the
physician should seek informed consent from the legally authorized representative. If no such representative is available
and if the research cannot be delayed, the study may proceed
without informed consent provided that the specific reasons
for involving subjects with a condition that renders them unable to give informed consent have been stated in the research
protocol and the study has been approved by a research ethics
committee. Consent to remain in the research should be obtained as soon as possible from the subject or a legally authorized representative.

Ethnically Publishing Results

Authors, editors and publishers all have ethical obligations with regard to the publication of the results of research. Authors have a duty to make publicly available the results of their research on human subjects and are accountable for the completeness and accuracy of their reports. They should adhere to accepted guidelines for ethical reporting. Negative and inconclusive as well as positive results should be published or otherwise made publicly available. Sources of funding, institutional affiliations and conflicts of interest should be declared in the publication. Reports of research not in accordance with the principles of this Declaration should not be accepted for publication.

The physician may combine medical research with medical care only to the extent that the research is justified by its potential preventive, diagnostic or therapeutic value and if the physician has good reason to believe that participation in the research study will not adversely affect the health of the patients who serve as research subjects.

The benefits, risks, burdens and effectiveness of a new intervention must be tested against those of the best current proven intervention, except in the following circumstances:

- The use of placebo, or no treatment, is acceptable in studies where no current proven intervention exists; or

- Where for compelling and scientifically sound methodological reasons the use of placebo is necessary to determine the efficacy or safety of an intervention and the patients who receive placebo or no treatment will not be subject to any risk of serious or irreversible harm. Extreme care must be taken to avoid abuse of this option.

Medical Care Combined with Medical Research

At the conclusion of the study, patients entered into the study are entitled to be informed about the outcome of the study and to share any benefits that result from it, for example, access to interventions identified as beneficial in the study or to other appropriate care or benefits.

The physician must fully inform the patient which aspects of the care are related to the research. The refusal of a patient to participate in a study or the patient's decision to withdraw from the study must never interfere with the patient-physician relationship.

In the treatment of a patient, where proven interventions do not exist or have been ineffective, the physician, after seeking expert advice, with informed consent from the patient or a legally authorized representative, may use an unproven intervention if in the physician's judgment it offers hope of saving life, re-establishing health or alleviating suffering. Where possible, this intervention should be made the object of research, designed to evaluate its safety and efficacy. In all cases, new information should be recorded and, where appropriate, made publicly available.

India Is a Prime Destination for Unethical Clinical Trials

Keya Acharya

In the following viewpoint, Keya Acharya reports on the growing concern in India over research and the number of clinical trials conducted in that country. Many large international companies are accused of illegal and unethical trials, according to Acharya. Of particular concern to scientists is the quality of stem cell research being conducted in India. According to the viewpoint, although India has made some attempts at regulating trials, there is still no body responsible for ethical oversight. Acharya is an environmental journalist from Bangalore, India.

As you read, consider the following questions:

1. What is the induced pluripotent stem cell method of research, and why is it a cause for ethical concern in Bernard Lo's opinion?

2. What did media coverage of the Johns Hopkins Hospital collaboration with the Regional Cancer Centre in Kerala force to happen, according to the viewpoint?

3. Who is setting up community advisory bodies to disseminate awareness and information on the rights of participants in clinical trials?

Keya Acharya, "Health-India: Prime Destination for Unethical Clinical Trials," IPS News, December 14, 2007. Reproduced by permission.

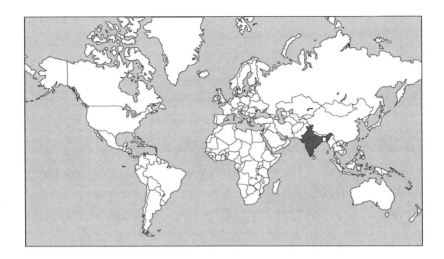

L ack of regulation, accountability, low costs of operation and wide availability of target participants are reasons why multinational drug companies, researchers and institutions are increasingly basing their clinical trials in India.

An estimated 40 percent of all clinical trials now take place in Asia, Eastern Europe, [and] Central and South America. "There is no compulsory registration system for clinical trials in these countries and many do not follow European directives in their operations", says Dr. Jacob Sijtsma of the Netherlands-based Wemos [Foundation], an advocacy health organisation tracking clinical trials in developing countries.

An estimated 40 percent of all clinical trials now take place in Asia, Eastern Europe, [and] Central and South America.

Sijtsma, who was in India for a bioethics conference, held [in 2007] at the Bangalore-based National Institute of Mental Health [and Neuro] Sciences, said there is a growing concern in India's medical and civil society on the lax regulation and ethicality over clinical trials conducted in this country.

Unethical Clinical Trials

In 2006, Wemos and the Centre for Research on Multinational Corporations prepared an overview of 22 known examples of unethical clinical trials, eight of which were operating in India.

The Indian examples of illegal and unethical trials involved Sun Pharmaceutical and Novartis's letrozole for inducing ovulation when approved only for breast cancer, Novo Nordisk's for diabetes treatment, Solvay Pharmaceuticals' for treating diarrhoea, Johnson & Johnson's for treating acute malaria, Pfizer's for cardiac events, Otsuka's for arterial disease, Indian companies Shantha Biotechnics and Biocon for diabetes and the Johns Hopkins University's trials for treating oral cancer.

Other countries with documented illegal trials include Russia, Nepal, Uganda, Peru, China, Nigeria, Argentina and even places like London and New York involving well-known institutes like the U.S. National Institutes of Health, Walter Reed Army Institute of Research, Centers for Disease Control [and Prevention] and several international pharmaceutical firms.

Stem Cell Research

Dr. Bernard Lo from the University of California at San Francisco, also here for the conference, said even more disturbing questions arise in the field of stem cell research in its newest method called induced pluripotent stem cell (iPS cells).

In this system, embryonic stem cells are not used, but virtually any cell is taken to the laboratory, inserted with a human gene and grown into human cells.

"This makes for laboratory manipulation of basic science research, no consent is needed by anyone and the cells can be bought commercially, giving rise to all sorts of ethical questions that need to keep pace with the rapid research in this field," said Lo.

"I am extremely concerned about the conduct of stem cell research in India," said Dr. Pushpa Bhargava, a highly respected former director of India's Centre for [Cellular and] Molecular Biology at Hyderabad city. "We have no idea where these cells are coming from, whether they have been characterised," Bhargava told IPS [a news agency].

"There is no method of validation or checking," he complained.

Secrecy Surrounds Trials

Wemos's Dr. Leontien Laterveer says a lack of transparency and secrecy shrouding all clinical trials, whether in India or other countries, makes it very difficult to obtain information about their operations.

"We are appealing to Indian organisations looking at this issue to come forward and collaborate with us," say both Laterveer and Sjitsma.

More importantly, there are insufficient checks by the European Union in spite of the Declaration of Helsinki [a statement of ethical principles for medical research] on a code of ethics for clinical trials, making it easy for drugs to enter the European market, add the two.

"European pharmaceuticals are also not bothered about legal and regulatory aspects," said Laterveer. "They leave it to the countries themselves." The Declaration of Helsinki is currently under review.

"We need the input of Southern experts to help process the review of the Helsinki Declaration," said Sjitsma.

Media exposés of exploitation in cases such as the U.S. Johns Hopkins Hospital's collaboration with the Regional Cancer Centre in Kerala, in 2000, forced the Indian Council of Medical Research (ICMR) to inquire into the trials.

The results however are still not public and no action has been taken against its then director, while the Johns Hopkins

Clinical Trials in Asia Are Rising Rapidly

India has shown a whopping 463.33% growth from 2002 to 2008 in terms of clinical trials registered to be conducted in India. China follows close second with a 365.56% rise in the same period. However, overall statistics showed that China remains number 1 for clinical trial destination amongst 5 countries.

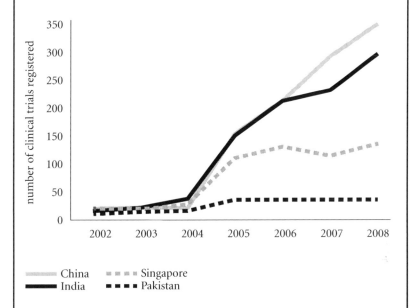

TAKEN FROM: Harit Mohan, "India Close Second to China in Clinical Trials Registered to Be Conducted in Asia: A Dolcera Study," July 7, 2009. blogs.dolcera.com/blog/2009/07/page/3/.

University barred the principal investigator from heading future research with human subjects.

In recent years, India has made some regulatory attempts, amending its drugs and cosmetics act to require compliance by trial conductors with a set of good clinical practices (GCP) guidelines along with the ethics committee that the ICMR formulated.

But there is still no mandatory compensatory payment, or strong penalty against the defaulting company.

Ethical Responsibility

"We need to pin down direct responsibility for monitoring with the ethics committee and measures taken to permanently revoke the licence of the defaulting company," says Adarsh Gangadhar, a lawyer attached to the National Academy for Legal Studies and Research in Hyderabad.

Dr. Prathap Tharyan, head of psychiatry at the respected Christian Medical College (CMC), Vellore, [India] and South Asia coordinator of Cochrane [Collaboration], a network of specialists working to improve evidence-based health care, averred that "deception, fraud and structural problems in randomised clinical trials" are rampant in India.

Tharyan has now helped set up an online clinical trials registry through ICMR. Its implementation, however, remains dependent on wider awareness of the issues involved in India.

"Ethics awareness in India is evolving and the law intervening, but I find a deficiency in working out solutions for implementation," said Madhava Menon, one of India's leading legal experts.

The National AIDS Research Institute (NARI) at Pune [India] is committed to setting up community advisory bodies (CABs) with participation from field workers, patients and others concerned to disseminate awareness and information on the rights of participants in clinical trials.

However, the entire concept of CABs is still evolving, with insufficient information on rights or ethical principles and no mechanism for redressal of grievances, NARI's Dr. Sanjay Mehendale told IPS.

In the Southern Hemisphere, Some AIDS Researchers Use Unethical Practices

Behzad Hassani

In the following viewpoint, Behzad Hassani notes that pharmaceutical companies look to nations in the Southern Hemisphere to recruit subjects for drug trials. He contends that many of these trials do not meet the criteria for ethical research. He highlights studies in Africa, Thailand, and other Asian countries where researchers tested AIDS drugs. Hassani further argues that using placebos, although producing scientifically valuable information, is not ethical since it denies some subjects effective treatment. Finally, he asserts that many studies violate the fundamental ethical pillar of medicine: care for the patient. Hassani is a medical doctor at the University of Toronto.

As you read, consider the following questions:

1. What three pillars of medical ethics were recognized by the Belmont Report in 1979?

2. What were the Tuskegee experiments and to what does Hassani compare them?

3. What situation does Hassani use as a clear example of a violation of the pillars of beneficence and nonmaleficence?

University of Toronto Medical Journal, vol. 82, no. 3, May 2005, pp. 212–215, for "Trials by Fire: The Case of Unethical Clinical Trials in the Countries of the South," by Behzad Hassani. Reproduced by permission of the publisher and author.

The journey of a new medication from laboratory bench to bedside and to the pharmacy shelf is, although profitable and prolonged, often arduous and troublesome. Traditionally, drugs are tested on animals first and then, in a series of phases that may take several years, on human subjects. Issues surrounding the ethics of human clinical trials have always been the source of much controversy, although such trials are regulated and governed by watchdogs in the developed countries (e.g., Food and Drug Administration in the USA). The story is somewhat different in the developing world.

A Shift of Focus

During recent years, the pharmaceutical corporations and their patrons in the biomedical profession and the public sector have faced several obstacles regarding the recruitment of human subjects and passing their proposals by ethical review boards. The rising competitive pressure on the companies to develop drugs and market them faster has naturally caused them to shift focus from the countries of [the] North to those of [the] South. This shift of focus is one of the most egregious and least examined manifestations of the neo-liberal globalization movement. Differential access to health care, lack of political resolve and the politico-economic hegemony of giant pharmaceutical companies in developing countries have allowed unethical drug testing to become a common and unopposed occurrence in the South. The ability of researchers to conduct unethical drug trials in developing countries is symptomatic of a greater calamity—the deep and dividing inequality between the countries of [the] North and [the] South that prescribes a monetary value to human life. Furthermore, as the director of marketing for Johnson & Johnson mentioned, foreign patients with little exposure to medicines "offer a blank slate for experimentation" as their medical deprivation makes for a scientifically sound study. This in turn speeds the journey of new drugs to the marketplace of the developed world. . . .

The Three Pillars of Medical Ethics

Most international guidelines governing the ethics of medical research were developed after World War II to safeguard the participants from exploitation and atrocities such as those committed by Nazi doctors in concentration camps. The Nuremberg war crimes tribunal laid down a series of ethical standards guiding the practice of medical research. Subsequent ethical guidelines built upon the principles rooted in Nuremberg Code. The Belmont Report[1] identified the three pillars of medical ethics: "respect for persons", that is recognizing individuals as autonomous and voluntary decision makers possessed of free will; "beneficence and non-maleficence" that is, ensuring the safety of the individuals by first causing no harm either through acts of commission or omission and by acting in the individual patient's best interest, an axiomatic concept in medicine; and "distributive justice", that is ensuring that the patients benefit from participating in the research and that care is equitably distributed among groups and individuals during and after the trials.

A critical extension of the principle of "respect for persons" and autonomy is the concept of informed consent. This ensures that the individual participating in the clinical trial is making the decision based on free will without coercion or outside influence, understands the risks involved, is aware of any potential benefits and their right to back out at any time. In the First World, it is vital that investigators obtain valid informed consent before patients take part in a trial. The repercussions for those who fail to uphold ethical principles in the North are stringent and can readily involve legal action. From an anthropological perspective, the above guidelines clearly reflect the individualistic ethos of Europe and North America, and thus constitute "ethnocentrism" when imposed upon other societies. Although, the pillars of beneficence, non-maleficence,

1. A 1979 statement of basic ethical principles governing research involving human subjects issued by the National Commission for the Protection of Human Subjects.

and justice may be deemed intuitive to the healer-patient relationship universally, problems are to be found with respect to the principle of autonomy and informed consent. . . .

Unethical AIDS Studies in Thailand

A series of articles in the year 2000 entitled the "Body Hunters", published in the *Washington Post*, were among the first to blow the whistle, revealing several unethical research practices in developing countries. This commendable journalistic effort by the *Washington Post* exposed the breach of moral codes in the work of several investigators conducting AIDS [acquired immune deficiency syndrome] studies in Thailand. Sponsored by the US Army, the experiments aimed to determine the natural course of vertical transmission of HIV [human immunodeficiency virus] from sero-positive mothers to infants through "monitoring". This approach did not call for the provision of the effective antiretroviral drug AZT to any of the participants. The trial was approved by the National Institutes of Health (NIH) before the widespread availability of AZT. A similar trial was being conducted simultaneously by researchers from Harvard University who felt that it would be unethical not to provide participants in the control group with AZT. Note that AZT had proven potent in diminishing the incidence of HIV vertical transmission in the US and France, and had been pronounced the standard treatment in the North prior to the Thai studies. The army researchers refused to allot some of their grant funding (a modest $1 million) to purchase AZT (cost of $15000). Not wanting to cooperate with the Harvard team (the army believed that cooperating with the Harvard team would have implied "surrendering the site"), army investigators decided to wait for the Thai government to provide the medication. The army argued that AZT was not deemed standard therapy in Thailand without Thai government's approval. Needless to say, the provision of AZT would have clouded the scientific validity of the study as it would have interfered with the "natural" transmission of HIV. 37 babies born to the HIV positive mothers, who could have been spared in the duration of study, contracted the virus. Thai government approved AZT several months prior to the conclusion of the above study; however, the provision of AZT was stalled through bureaucratic means, lest the scientific purity of the research be corrupted by the medication. In response to criticism from several ethic review boards, the team leader expressed his disappointment with the boards as "their deliberations seem often devoid of the larger view of advancing medical science for public good as opposed to the individual."

The Tuskegee Experiments

It appears that on the path to scientific glory, the prosperous North contributes genius, hypotheses, and capital while the South provides vast numbers of chemically uncorrupted patients. In this global village, we live in a climate of *belief* in which the safety of persons, particularly those of darker hues and lower socioeconomic status, is considered inferior to the health of the whiter and more prosperous population. The Western tradition of intellectual endeavor and information gathering, in brief the realm of the intelligentsia, is believed to be superior to the traditional subsistence-driven labour (i.e., the "primitive endeavor"). The health of the South is deemed secondary to the advancement of science. With this bitter reality in mind, I ask the reader to compare the case discussed above with the infamous Tuskegee experiment below. Have we truly progressed?

The Tuskegee experiments were conducted by the US government on black farmworkers in the US from 1932 to 1972. The investigators' prerogative was to monitor the natural course of syphilis infection without the provision of treatment. Although penicillin, still the most effective therapy for syphilis, became available in 1943, the investigators did not provide the drug to their patients after its introduction, and in fact actively dissuaded them from pursuing the treatment option for 30 years. This was done so that the treatment "would not cloud the scientific validity" of the study of "Untreated Syphilis in the Negro Male". The Tuskegee experiments were stopped due to public outrage after front-page reports in the *New York Times* exposed this inherently racist, demoralizing, and dehumanizing medicine. In 1997, President Clinton offered formal apologies to the survivors of these experiments and called the studies "blight on our record."

The striking parallels between Tuskegee and the Thai study are disturbingly clear. The very unequal distribution of power in the doctor-patient interactions is facilitated by the lower socioeconomic status of participants of color, scientific egotism, and a medical orthodoxy with a racist past. This past is perpetuated in the present. Tuskegee may never be repeated in the USA again, yet this blight on North's record continues. Tuskegee has been exported to the developing world.

Unethical AIDS Trials in Asia and Africa

Another disturbing series of trials conducted in 1996 under the auspices of the National Institutes of Health (NIH) and Centers for Disease Control [and Prevention] (CDC) in several Asian and African countries sought to assess the efficacy of shorter courses of AZT in preventing mother-child transmission of HIV among 17000 HIV-positive women. A longer regimen of AZT had already been proven effective in the USA and France, and the researchers had decided to devise a shorter, simpler, and cheaper regimen that would be suitable for breastfeeding women in resource-poor countries. The endeavor was proclaimed a "humanitarian venture." Of the two groups of female participants, one received AZT, but in a shorter course, for fewer weeks, and was administered doses less frequently than was the standard in the US regimen. The newborns would receive no AZT, unlike American infants who had received AZT for six weeks after birth. The other group would receive a placebo implying that the children born to the sero-positive mothers of the placebo group would contract the virus. The CDC and NIH defended their methods by asserting that a placebo-controlled trial (PCT) offered the most resource-efficient and expeditious method of obtaining scientifically rigorous results, hence speeding the delivery of the regimen to the patients of the developing world. They further argued that the researchers were not required to provide the best medical care possible (i.e., the longer AZT regimen of the North) since such care was not the standard of the developing countries. The use of placebos, therefore, did not deny patients the care to which they would otherwise have access. [M.H.] Kottow argued against the double standards by pointing out that even in the North, there are many "pockets" of impoverished people with little or no access to health care. Even though these groups resemble populations of the South, researchers are required under ethical codes to offer the best possible medical care to them. The same must be applied to people of the South.

The Placebo Debate

The pro-placebo arguments were further criticized by Drs. [Peter] Lurie and [Sidney M.] Wolfe of Public Citizen, a US-based public watchdog. They asserted that in the South, patients cannot benefit from the advanced regimens due to economic constraints imposed by the high prices set by the pharmaceutical companies. They further noted that such unavailability is certainly not because the Third World's medical authorities have assessed the regimens to be ineffective and hence refused to approve them as standard of care. Since researchers often receive free samples of the drugs they are testing from the manufacturers, they are denying patients the chance to receive the care which is at their disposal. They further contended that equivalency trials, which utilize the best-

Number of Medical Studies by Region

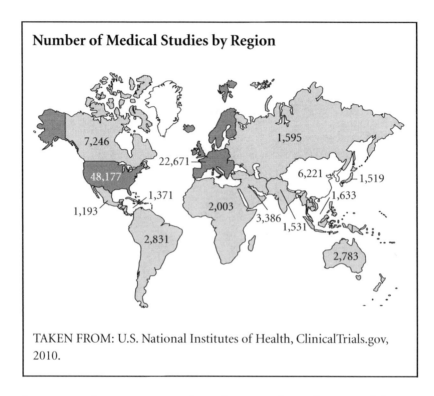

TAKEN FROM: U.S. National Institutes of Health, ClinicalTrials.gov, 2010.

known regimen compared against another plan, would provide data as valid, if not more accurate, than the PCT.

In fact, such an alternative was explored simultaneously in a study undertaken by Harvard University researchers who examined how different doses of AZT influenced transmission rates. Notice that the equivalency study received funding from the NIH only after a bitter battle was fought between Harvard scientists (who contended that a placebo-controlled trial was unethical when an effective treatment was available) and the NIH who emphasized the use of placebos for scientific accuracy. In essence, this alternative would pose the question "Is this treatment as good as, or nearly as good as, the accepted standard treatment?" compared to the placebo question "Is this treatment better than nothing?" I contend that it is unethical to even ask whether X is better than nothing when one knows that a Y exists that is very much better than nothing.

The proponents of PCT asserted that the longer AZT regimen could not be implemented in the developing world where women are often malnourished, anemic, and harboring infections other than HIV. They noted that the longer AZT regimen requires that newborns be bottle-fed, an obstacle in the South where breastfeeding is the norm. In fact, they accused their critics of "ethical imperialism" since they demanded that the ethical standards which evolved in the North be applied without flexibility to research universally. [H.] Varmus and [D.] Satcher, the heads of public institutes of NIH and CDC respectively, called the position taken by the critics "absurd" and sarcastically claimed that implementation of the equivalency studies would require making radical changes to the prenatal care programs in these countries: cleaning up the water supply and stocking up on ample amounts of baby formula and food for the mothers. They further threatened that the drug donors in the pharmaceutical industry would not back these studies, let alone the continued post-trial treatment from which they stand to gain no profit.

Conduct of [medical] trials in the countries of [the] South cannot be proclaimed "humanitarian" or ethical if the conditions and goals of the studies are not adapted to the local health infrastructures of the communities.

Researchers Must Help Communities

I concur that the practicalities of providing the Northern regimen in the Southern countries with a poorly developed health infrastructure are daunting. For this very reason, I argue that the conduct of such trials in the countries of [the] South cannot be proclaimed "humanitarian" or ethical if the conditions and goals of the studies are not adapted to the local health infrastructures of the communities. US scientists change these communities merely by setting up drug trials, as they temporarily introduce higher levels of care and thus are bound by the pillar of distributive justice to help the communities after the trials end. If the regimen proves effective, the investigators must ensure that the local governments take steps towards implementing the prevention program. Otherwise, the women who received placebos have been doubly harmed.

Needless to say, the beneficent North also benefits from these "humanitarian" trials. If the tested regimen is effective, the corporations reap financial benefits, and if the regimen is of little value, individuals in the North will not be subjected to the potential risks of the trials.

Adherence to scientific orthodoxy must not be used as justification to evade the duty of care, the core pillar of medicine.

Violating the Ethical Pillars

On the ethical front, I contend that one cannot morally conduct an HIV test on an expectant mother, fully disclose the positive status to the patient who has no access to proper care except for what the scientists may provide, and yet refuse to provide at least some care for the mother and the unborn baby. The women and their unborn children were harmed by not receiving the available treatment. This was a clear violation of the pillars of beneficence and non-maleficence. Yet I believe that the matter is further complicated by the fact that even the women who received the prophylactic [preventative] treatment did not benefit directly—only their future offspring did. According to the pillar of distributive justice, the women themselves must also receive treatments for their disease. One wonders what will become of the children who are saved by AZT therapy. When their mothers succumb to AIDS, will they become part of the burgeoning population of AIDS orphans with limited survival prospects?

In the above case study, the gross inequity in resources, particularly concerning health care provision, which exists between the affluent industrialized nations and the developing countries, is once again apparent. The controversy has demonstrated the waning prenatal care and high infant mortality rates of the South. It has revealed the markedly disparate fates of HIV-infected pregnant women in the North versus those in the South. Furthermore, it has highlighted the vulnerability of women in certain cultures and the lack of choices available to them in terms of contraception, protection from HIV infection, and infant feeding. On a more philosophical note, the debate has manifested the tension between the modernist ethics of science, grounded in an orthodox "mechanistic-reductionist paradigm" and an ethic based on a more "humanistic, post-modern paradigm." The former is apparent in the PCT which strives to create order and predictability in the entropic world of complexity and uncertainty. Although the PCT may provide us with "hard unbiased" evidence, it also sacrifices the human concerns, needs, preferences, and relationships. In doing so, it demolishes the variables that compel humans to act as moral agents to one another. Such rigid scientific adherence to objectivity necessitates even more robust ethical safeguards in order to protect the vulnerable from exploitation. The post-modern ethic, on the other hand, allows for the human voice to be heard and embraces the inherent uncertainty of science. I believe that adherence to scientific orthodoxy must not be used as justification to evade the duty of care, the core pillar of medicine. By evading this duty, the North sets dangerous precedents and paves the way to further negligence of "reverence for life" on a global scale.

The Japanese Government Tightens Ethical Guidelines for Medical Research

Koji Masuda

In the following viewpoint, Koji Masuda reports on a plan by the Japanese Ministry of Health, Labour and Welfare to strengthen ethics regulations in medical studies. The decision comes after a survey conducted by a national newspaper revealed the majority of ethics committees were not following established guidelines, according to Masuda. The new regulations will expand the government's monitoring system of medical trials and increase surveillance of ethical issues. Institutions and researchers operating outside the ethical guidelines will face punishment. Masuda is a staff writer for the Yomiuri Shimbun *newspaper.*

As you read, consider the following questions:

1. What are the two main points of the ethical guidelines revisions, according to the viewpoint?

2. What were two violations of ethical guidelines the survey by the *Yomiuri Shimbun* uncovered?

3. According to the viewpoint, about how many clinical study programs receive government subsidies annually?

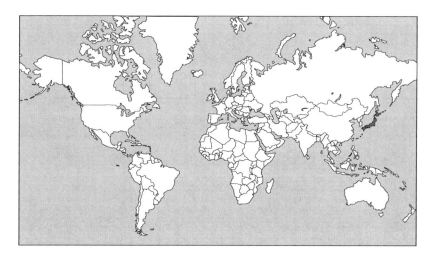

The [Japanese] Health, Labour and Welfare Ministry is to toughen procedures to protect the health and human rights of test subjects in clinical studies, following a high incidence of violations by medical institutions of its ethical guidelines.

By revising the guidelines, the ministry also plans to beef up its surveillance of clinical research irregularities.

The planned revisions, which follow a year of scrutiny of the issue, indicate the ministry's resolve to ensure ethics in clinical studies, which are crucial to progress in medical science and treatments.

Reflecting a sense of urgency, the ministry will put the revised guidelines into force in April [2009], two months earlier than planned.

The main points of the revisions will:

- Obligate medical research institutions to report annually to the government details of the activities of their ethics committees, which scrutinize the validity of the organizations' clinical studies.

- Make the self-evaluation by research institutions of clinical tests' ethical validity mandatory.

In addition, the new guidelines will boost greatly the ministry's powers to check violators, through on-the-spot investigations or by checking relevant documents. Medical research institutions that violate the revised guidelines will be subject to punitive measures such as suspension of government clinical research subsidies.

Why Stronger Guidelines Are Necessary

Why are stronger guidelines necessary?

This question spotlights the highly precarious state of affairs involving clinical studies.

Clinical studies, in which humans are used as test subjects, can cause unexpected health consequences, including death.

To minimize such risks, research institutions' ethics committees have been responsible for judging whether a given clinical research project should be considered worth undertaking as well as the permissibility of probable risks to the test subjects.

In addition, the subjects' informed consent must be secured prior to the research.

The guidelines in their current form have made these procedures compulsory, but sufficient compliance remains a problem.

The *Yomiuri Shimbun* [a Japanese newspaper] has conducted a nationwide fact-finding survey last year [2007] on the ethics committees of hospitals that are certified by the ministry as advanced treatment facilities as well as those operated by medical departments of universities.

The survey was aimed at determining whether the ethics committees surveyed were operating in compliance with the guidelines.

The result was astonishing: A great majority of the ethics committees polled were found to be violating the guidelines. Many of the committees failed to have minimum numbers of female members or staff from outside the medical institutions.

Some of the committees admitted they had allowed medical doctors seeking approval for clinical test projects to be present at the committee deliberations in violation of the guidelines.

It was revealed in July 2007 that the Kobe municipal hospital had been carrying out clinical studies of a new cancer medicine without obtaining the advance consent of the patients involved.

For example, it was revealed in July 2007 that the Kobe municipal hospital had been carrying out clinical studies of a new cancer medicine without obtaining the advance consent of the patients involved.

The ministry's decision to revise the ethics guidelines to ensure compliance, while creating punitive steps such as suspending research subsidies, reflects the need to protect the human rights and safety of test subjects. It also comes amid recently surging awareness among patients of their rights.

Japanese Ethics Committees Must Be Improved

Ministry officials say they are determined to improve without delay the way ethics committees operate.

Until now, the effectiveness of such bodies has left much to be desired.

The ethics screening process for clinical studies requires the collaboration of experts from various fields, including health care ethics and law.

However, most medical institutions' ethics screening panels badly lack such expert personnel, leaving them far from the goal of securing the specialists in a systematic manner.

Japan Lags Behind in Medical Research

[Japan's] performance in the area of health and medical research compares unfavourably with many of its peers. Fortunately, the Japanese government . . . has initiated significant reforms. . . .

In Japan, health and medical research is performed largely by universities and private industry. . . . Public research institutes play a smaller but significant role within the system. Funding for these players comes from private industry, which funds its own research activities, and government, which provides the vast majority of funding to the universities and research institutes through its education and health ministries. The central government also oversees the national university system, as well as the development of drugs and medical devices.

Unfortunately, a lack of communication between the academic and private sectors has hindered Japan's industrial success in the area of health and medical research. Universities in particular have been criticised for being too rigid and unresponsive to the nation's economic and health needs: too often, the innovative discoveries of Japan's universities have not been applied or commercialised. Meanwhile, Japan's relative level of investment in this area of research lags behind other nations. . . .

The pharmaceutical industry also faces serious difficulties related to the high costs and slow pace of development, and a declining share of domestic and global markets. Recognising the problems, the government has reformed the universities, . . . and has introduced new incentives for cooperation with industry.

James R. Burgdorf, Health and Medical Research in Japan,
RAND Europe Health Research Observatory, 2008, pp. vii–viii.

The *Yomiuri* survey last year brought to light the difficulty many medical institutions have experienced in trying to ensure the composition of their ethics committees fits in with the guidelines.

It may be unreasonable for the ministry to pressure medical research institutions to comply with the guidelines without paying heed to the hardships most medical institutions have encountered.

There also is the question of whether the ministry will be able to perform its envisioned surveillance of medical institutions.

Investigative Ethical Surveillance Teams Are Understaffed

The ministry plans to bolster its monitoring system by spring, but indications are that its surveillance team will comprise less than 10 officials.

Can that number of officials be sufficient to investigate clinical study programs receiving government subsidies, which total about 400 annually nationwide?

Can it be considered adequate to omit a large number of clinical studies that are not covered by government subsidies and therefore not subject to the ministry's ethics surveillance?

Compared with medical ethics surveillance systems in the United States and Europe, which involve scores of officials, Japan's system cannot be called anything but feeble.

The government's planned surveillance-strengthening measures can serve the additional positive purpose of enhancing a sense of deep concern on the part of medical institutions and researchers over medical ethics.

But as long as the government fails to secure an environment conducive to medical institutions' compliance with the ethics guidelines and establish an effective surveillance system, a lack of mutual trust between the government and medical institutions is likely to grow.

In the United States, Ethicists Debate Using Prison Inmates for Medical Testing

Timothy J. Wiegand

In the following viewpoint, Timothy J. Wiegand traces the history of pharmaceutical research on prisoners, noting that current regulations were created as a result of the Tuskegee experiments on untreated syphilis in black farmworkers. At present, there is a strong push to expand the use of prisoners as clinical test subjects, according to Wiegand. Many ethicists and medical personnel fear this will lead to unethical treatment of prisoners and violate their rights. Other scientists, however, believe the benefit to the greater population outweighs any potential prisoner abuse. Wiegand is an internist and toxicologist in Portland, Maine.

As you read, consider the following questions:

1. Until the early 1970s, what percentage of pharmaceutical testing was carried out on prison inmates, according to federal officials?
2. Why does Wiegand say the existing lack of medical services for prisoner test subjects raises ethical concerns?
3. What medical breakthroughs as a result of testing on prisoners does Albert Kligman cite?

Timothy J. Wiegand, "Captive Subjects: Pharmaceutical Testing and Prisoners," *Journal of Medical Toxicology*, vol. 3, no. 1, March 2007, pp. 37–38. Reproduced by permission.

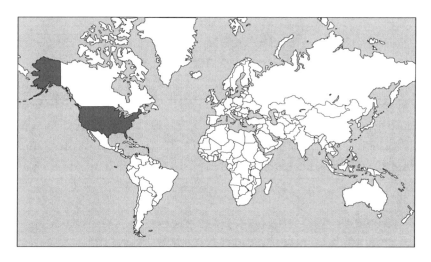

The debate about using prison inmates for medical testing has again surfaced. A federal panel of medical advisors from the Institute of Medicine (IOM) of the National Academy of Sciences has recommended that the government loosen restrictions limiting testing of pharmaceutical agents on prisoners. Current [2007] regulations, passed in 1978, allow prison inmates to participate in federally financed biomedical research if the experiments pose no more than "minimal" risks to the subjects. The IOM report advises, however, that experiments with greater risk be permitted if they have the potential to benefit prisoners. Additionally, while current regulations only cover federally funded prison research, the new recommendations also advise the inclusion of privately funded research. The new recommendations would include individuals on probation and parole—increasing the overall number of "prisoners" [a]ffected by these regulations from 2 million to nearly 7 million.

Current Regulations

The current regulations (regarding the use of prisoners as subjects in pharmaceutical research) were created in response to revelations of harmful and coercive practices that occurred in prison research conducted during the 1950s and through 1970. This was a period of increased awareness of abuse in prisons, and with it came revelations regarding the treatment of the subjects in the "Tuskegee Study of Untreated Syphilis in the Negro Male." The climate was right for increased oversight and regulation. A recent *New York Times* editorial, written in response to the IOM report, further discusses this context and highlights specific instances and institutions where abuse was rampant.

> Until the early 1970s about 90 percent of all pharmaceutical products were tested on prison inmates, federal officials say. But such research diminished sharply in 1974 after revelations of abuse at prisons like Holmesburg here *(highlighted in the* New York Times *article)*, where inmates were paid hundreds of dollars a month to test items as varied as dandruff treatments and dioxin, and where they were exposed to radioactive, hallucinogenic and carcinogenic chemicals.

Historically, isolated and sporadic episodes of the use of prisoners as study subjects for pharmaceutical research existed before World War II, yet it was wartime medical projects that fully launched prison-based research. In 1944 hundreds of prisoners in the state of Illinois consented to infection with malaria as researchers searched for new and more effective ways to prevent and treat tropical diseases that ravaged the Allied forces in the Pacific. In response to these experiments, a committee was created to analyze the ethics of prisoners as research subjects. This committee subsequently pronounced the experiments "ideal" in their conformity to the American Medical Association (AMA) rules concerning human experimentation. The findings, then, were published in the nation's leading medical journal, the *Journal of the American Medical Association* (JAMA). This publication signified acceptance of prison-based research by the medical community. After this publication the use of prisoners in research gained such momentum that (until the early 1970s) nearly all trials involving investigational new drugs were conducted on prisoners.

The Demand for Clinical Trials

Currently, there is a significant demand for pharmaceutical testing. From 1995 to 2005, the contract research industry, grown out of the increasing need for subject recruitment for clinical trials, has grown from a 1 billion to a 7 billion dollar-per-year industry. Along with increasing testing needs has come high-profile cases of drug toxicity, and these cases have created increased public awareness about the need for study and surveillance of drug toxicity. For example, it has been suggested that increased testing of Vioxx would have prevented the delay in discovering its cardiovascular toxicity.

Despite calls for increased testing, the pharmaceutical industry was not involved in prompting the IOM recommendations. Interestingly, even prior to the FDA's [Food and Drug Administration's] proposal in the 1970s regarding a change in regulations for using prisoners in drug testing, the pharmaceutical industry was turning to the private sector for subject recruitment. They found sufficient numbers of experimental subjects by recruiting students and the poor. The growing controversy regarding the ethics of prisoner use also influenced their decision, yet it was mainly expediency and not the ethical considerations that influenced their decision. In an advisory committee on human experiments report regarding pharmaceutical research in prisoners, an administrator associated with an Eli Lilly testing operation at an Indiana prison stated the "reason [they] closed the doggone thing down was that [they] were getting too much hassle and heat from the press. It just didn't seem worth it."

Although the current recommendations call for expanded use of prisoners in research, the IOM authors say they have also written safeguards into their recommendations that will prevent past abuses from occurring in the future. One change recommended by authors of the IOM report allows for prisoners to take part in federally financed clinical trials that only occur in the later, safer, clinical phases. They also recommend that at least half of the subjects in any given trial be non-prisoners, thus allowing for parity in the recruitment to test products that may be more "frightening" to volunteers. Finally, where current research in prisons is only regulated if funded federally—under the proposed regulations all research using prison inmates (regardless of the funding) would be regulated.

From 1995 to 2005, the contract research industry, grown out of the increasing need for subject recruitment for clinical trials, has grown from a 1 billion to a 7 billion dollar-per-year industry.

The Potential for Abuse

Although the proposed changes include provisions intended to prevent the abuses that plagued the previous programs, many prison rights advocates worry that the system would continue to be fraught with potential for abuse. Central to this concern is the debate regarding whether prisoners can truly make uncoerced decisions. The role of financial remuneration in this process raises concerns. When prisoners can earn up to $1500.00 a month by participating in pharmaceutical research, and the only other jobs pay 15 to 25 cents a day, officials are concerned this establishes a coercive environment. As evidence for concern, prisoner advocates cite the shortages of basic medical necessities in prison medical facilities. If prisoners cannot get basic necessities like antibiotics or high blood pressure medication, it seems foolish to suggest that they would benefit from access to cutting-edge therapy and expensive medications by consenting to serve as research subjects. In this resource-poor environment, prisoner advocates worry that prisoners may simply enroll in research to gain access to

Prisoners as Human Subjects: Ethical Ambiguity

Clinical research involving prisoners as human subjects may be an important undertaking. Prison populations are characterized by many problems involving the human condition, including poor health status, with the prevalence of many of these problems significantly higher among prisoners than among non-prisoners. . . . Research may yield valuable information about the nature of the health and well-being of persons who are incarcerated. . . .

However, history has demonstrated that research involving prisoners implicates some of the most troubling ethical issues of our time. The forcible use of concentration camp prisoners as research subjects by Nazi (German) scientists and physicians, and the coerced use of prisoners as subjects by U.S. scientists and federal and state governments, are considered among the most egregious cases of widespread abuse of human subjects of research in modern history.

This history has had a profound effect upon the way in which research involving prisoners is viewed by society, and has, in no small part, helped to inform the development of various ethical norms and principles pertaining to human subject protection, including protection of prisoners as research subjects. Not unexpectedly, federal—and to a lesser extent, certain state—laws now incorporate some of these norms. Nonetheless, these laws and their underlying rationale are not always clear or unambiguous. To complicate matters, their application in practice is often subject to varying interpretation or even misunderstanding. . . .

T. Howard Stone, Prisoners as Human Subjects: Clinical Researcher Reference Guide, *2004, pp. 6–7.*

the medical system. California, with some of the nation's largest prisons (which have been subject to severe overcrowding), has already announced that it will not allow the use of prisoners in experiments. Some scientists and physicians who participated in the previous experiments agree, and they worry that any access into the prison system produces an environment ripe for abuse. Even though suggested regulations provide for increased oversight of prisoners involved in clinical trials, some scientists worry that free and informed consent remains a valid issue.

While prisoner rights are central to the debate, oversight remains a significant concern. In 2000, several universities were reprimanded for their use of federal money after conducting hundreds of projects on prisoners but not fully reporting the experiments to the appropriate officials. Many are concerned that supervision, while difficult to conduct in the current environment, would be even more difficult with additional freedom to perform clinical research on prisoners.

When prisoners can earn up to $1500.00 a month by participating in pharmaceutical research and the only other jobs pay 15 to 25 cents a day, officials are concerned this establishes a coercive environment.

The Benefits to Public Health

Other scientists do not share this belief; however, they believe the benefit to public health outweighs any risk for abuse. Dr. Albert Kligman, currently an emeritus professor of dermatology at the University of Pennsylvania Medical School [Penn] and former director of the experiments at Holmesburg Prison, is quoted in the *New York Times* article. He cites breakthroughs such as Retin-A—an anti-acne drug, and ingredients for the creams and salves to treat poison ivy as evidence of public benefits from prison studies. While confirming that various dangerous substances were used on prisoners during his days as director of experiments at Holmesburg Prison, he believes that substances were always administered in low doses and in a careful manner so as to minimize harm. A current member of the ethics committee at Penn, he has stated that he still does not see "anything wrong with what [they] were doing."

Interestingly, the use of prisoners as research subjects has been mostly an American phenomenon. Other countries basically did away with this practice after the development of the Nuremburg Code.[1] The first clause of the Nuremberg Code begins with the assertion that the only acceptable experimental subjects are those who are "so situated as to be able to exercise free power of choice." From abroad, it is viewed that the United States has a fairly loose interpretation of this clause.

Ernest D. Prentice, chair of the Department of Health and Human Services' advisory committee, discusses the impact of the IOM recommendations in a *Philadelphia Inquirer* article. He says that changes, if any, are still a long time coming. What remains to be seen is whether we can learn from the mistakes of the past.

---

1. A set of research ethics principles for human experimentation established at the end of World War II.

In Singapore, Ethicists Rule in Favor of Donating Human Eggs for Research Purposes

Lim Pin et al.

In the following viewpoint, Lim Pin and the members of the Bioethics Advisory Committee (BAC) of Singapore outline the ethical considerations concerning the donation of human eggs for research purposes. The BAC bases its judgments on these principles: respect for individuals, reciprocity, proportionality, justice, and sustainability. The committee recommends that healthy women can ethically donate eggs so long as they freely consent to the procedure and are well informed as to the risks. The BAC also stipulates that no payment can be given to the woman. Pin is the chair of the Singapore Bioethics Advisory Committee, a governmentally appointed body charged with ethical rulings on medical issues.

As you read, consider the following questions:

1. What does the voluntary nature of contributing tissue for research mandate, according to the viewpoint?
2. What is one safeguard against the exploitation of prospective egg donors?
3. According to the viewpoint, the BAC is sensitive to the great importance attributed to what institution?

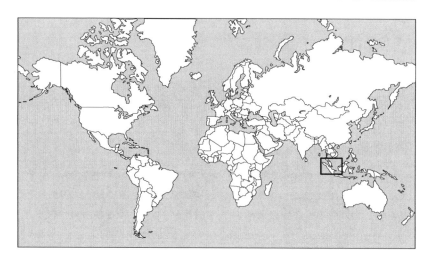

Certain ethical principles have formed the basis of the BAC's [Bioethics Advisory Committee's] recommendations in its various reports. These can be summarised as follows:

(a) *Respect for individuals*. The autonomy of individuals is to be respected, and their welfare and interests are to be protected, especially when their ability to exercise their autonomy is impaired or lacking. This principle underscores the importance of informed consent, respect for privacy, safeguarding confidentiality, and it also entails a proper regard for religious and cultural diversity;

(b) *Reciprocity*. The BAC has interpreted the idea of reciprocity between the individual and the wider society as an expression of the well-established idea that there is some implicit recognition of mutual obligation that regulates the relationship between the individual and society. In biomedical research, agreed social benefits— as a public good—carry an implication that, if accepted, they inherently reflect an in-principle willingness to consider participation in research of the kind yielding the accepted benefits. This means that there is -

a balance to be struck between the interests of the public and the rights of individual participants, and that incompatible and irreconcilable ethical perspectives should be resolved with regards to the public interest;

(c) *Proportionality.* The regulation of research should be in proportion to the possible threats to autonomy, welfare or public good;

(d) *Justice.* The idea of justice as applied to research includes the general principle of fairness and equality under the law. This implies that access to the benefits of publicly funded research, and the burden of supporting it, should be equitably shared in society. It also implies that researchers incur a responsibility for the welfare of participants and their possible compensation or treatment in the event of adverse outcomes arising directly from their participation; and

(e) *Sustainability.* The research process should be sustainable, in the sense that it should not jeopardise or prejudice the welfare of later generations. For example, research leading to permanent change to the human genome would not be considered ethical, on the grounds that the long-term implications are unforeseeable and might not be beneficial.

Intrinsic to the principle of respect for individuals is the requirement that potential egg donors should freely decide whether or not to contribute eggs for research.

It is important to ensure that human eggs for research are obtained in a manner based on internationally accepted ethical principles and practices. The general principles for research involving human participants will ordinarily apply, although there are certain issues, such as informed consent and compensation, that need special consideration. In addition, caution must be taken to ensure that no one is exploited, especially vulnerable individuals who are financially disadvantaged or in dependent relationships. . . .

Recommendations for the Regulation of Research

The procurement and use of human eggs for research should be regulated.

A number of respondents to the BAC's public consultation emphasised that researchers should respect the privacy concerns of donors and safeguard any confidential information that has been entrusted to them. The BAC is in agreement and reiterates its view that personal information that is used in research should be de-identified as far and as early as possible, and should be stored or transferred as de-identified information.

Intrinsic to the principle of respect for individuals is the requirement that potential egg donors should freely decide whether or not to contribute eggs for research. Their consent must be given without coercion or inducement, and on the basis of information that is sufficient and appropriately presented. Potential donors should also be provided with adequate time to make an informed decision. In addition, they should be informed that they have the right to withdraw consent or vary the terms of consent at any time before their eggs are actually used in research.

To ensure that a potential donor is fully informed before making a decision to donate eggs for research, the consent-taking process should include the following information, insofar as applicable:

(a) the purpose and nature of the research;

(b) the procedures and possible health risks;

(c) the possibility of a reduced chance of achieving pregnancy;

(d) that the research may not have any direct benefit to her, as any potential benefit can only be realised in the future and is for the public good;

(e) the ways in which her privacy and the confidentiality of her personal information will be safeguarded;

(f) whether the donated eggs may be used to create embryos for research, which will thus be destroyed during the process;

(g) whether the derived cells will be kept for future research that is not predictable at the present time;

(h) whether she may be re-contacted regarding the future use of her eggs, e.g., for the creation of gametes, or for research into therapeutic applications where the personal information of the donor needs to be retained;

(i) whether the eggs or derived cells may be used for research involving genetic manipulation;

(j) that eggs used for stem cell research will not be used to produce a pregnancy, and will not be allowed to develop *in vitro* for more than 14 days;

(k) whether the results of the research will be conveyed to her;

(l) the disclosure of any expected possible commercial benefit;

(m) that she has the right to withdraw consent or vary the terms of her consent at any time before her eggs are actually used in research, how she may withdraw consent and the implications of any withdrawal; and

(n) whether and how she will be compensated for her donation.

Issues Surrounding Donor Consent

A potential donor needs to be reassured that any current or prospective benefit, or medical care will not be affected if she decides not to consent. This is especially true if she is in a dependent relationship, where caution may be necessary. In a situation where the risk of coercion, inducement or undue influence cannot be avoided, the donation should not be accepted. For instance, it would be ethically inappropriate for principal investigators to accept the donation of eggs by members of their research team, due to a serious risk of undue influence.

The voluntary nature of contributing tissue for research mandates that there should be no pressure on women undergoing IVF [in vitro fertilisation] treatment to donate eggs out of a sense of obligation to their attending physicians. The free and informed nature of consent should be ensured, and this entails avoiding any conflicts of interest in the process of taking consent. . . .

Consent for the donation of human eggs for research should be obtained without any coercion or inducement. Potential donors must be provided with sufficient information in an understandable form, and given adequate time to make an informed decision.

Donors should be informed that they have the right to withdraw consent or vary the terms of consent any time before their eggs are actually used in research.

Consent for the donation of eggs for research from women undergoing fertility treatment should be taken independently of the treatment team. The donors should confirm in writing that they do not require these eggs for future reproductive use.

Egg Donation by Healthy Women

It is ethically acceptable for informed and consenting healthy women not undergoing fertility treatment to donate eggs for research. The principle of respect for individuals (and their autonomy in decision making) supports this, and it is already the legal position in Singapore. The public consultation that

---

Why Human Eggs Are in Short Supply

One of the outcomes of biotechnological progress is that human cells, tissues and organs have become valuable as commodities which can be bought and sold. For this reason, when certain human body parts become desirable—and by their nature are normally of limited availability—there are market pressures that turn them into (potential—if policy will allow it) premium commodities.

Human oocytes [eggs] are valuable, because they are necessary for human reproduction—and therefore can become a commodity in the reproductive 'business', which is currently driven by higher levels of infertility and women choosing to have children later in life—but they are also valuable as a research resource. These dual demands, plus other issues such as health risks in donation and the removal of donor anonymity, mean that oocytes are in short supply. The two main areas of research that require oocytes are fertility-related research and stem cell (SC) research. It is the latter research—driven by both hype and hope—that will predictably create the greatest demand for oocytes in research.

Benjamin Capps,
"Oocyte Procurement for Research,"
Background Paper for the Bioethics
Advisory Committee of Singapore, April 2007.

---

was recently conducted by the BAC indicated that the general public is mostly supportive of this position, provided that donors are counselled to ensure their donation is genuinely informed and voluntary, and that there are effective safeguards against exploitation.

One safeguard against exploitation is the requirement by the MOH [Ministry of Health] for all prospective egg donors for research to be provided with comprehensive information and be interviewed by a three-member panel before ovarian stimulation begins. The panel, which may be from the hospital's ethics committee, consists of a lay person and 2 medical practitioners, one of whom must be an authorised assisted reproduction practitioner. The panel must be satisfied that the prospective donor is of sound mind, clearly understands the nature and consequences of the donation, and has freely given explicit consent, without any inducement, coercion or undue influence. Even with this process, much vigilance is required as there is no perfect safeguard against the threat of exploitation. Members of the public have raised a number of considerations during the public consultation which may be helpful. These include giving due regard to the donors' residential and financial status, and their age and educational level. It was proposed that the number of times that donation may be made should be set by the regulating authority. The BAC is of the view that safeguards in the consent-taking process should be reviewed from time to time to ensure that they remain effective.

It is ethically acceptable for informed and consenting healthy women not undergoing fertility treatment to donate eggs for research.

Non-Commercialisation of the Human Body

A central ethical concern arising from obtaining human eggs for research relates to the possible commercialisation of the human body. The current view in research and clinical practice alike, is that the commercialisation of human tissues is not desirable, as it conflicts with a principle of respect for individuals. It is for this reason that blood donors, for example, are not paid but make a voluntary contribution to the public good. An egg donor, on this view, should not be motivated by any financial incentive in making the donation, although reasonable reimbursement of expenses incurred may be given.

The Human Cloning and Other Prohibited Practices Act of 2005 gives legal effect to this ethical principle, specifying that a person is prohibited from giving or receiving valuable consideration for the supply of human eggs, or to otherwise make an offer to that effect. "Valuable consideration" includes "any inducement, discount or priority in the provision of a service to the person, but does not include the payment of reasonable expenses incurred by the person in connection with the supply."

The BAC maintains that when tissue is donated for research, it should be an outright gift. This implies that the donor does not retain rights over the donated tissue (including eggs) or the results of research done using it. However, a donor can express a view as to the type of research that may or may not be done with the donated material. Donors can always decline to donate if any restrictions they wish to place on the research are not acceded to, and this matter should be addressed during the process of consent taking.

Current ethical thinking in Singapore . . . supports a view that financial inducement to provide an organ or tissue would amount to a form of commercialisation and is not acceptable.

Respect for the human body has always been seen as fundamental to ethical thinking and conduct in both medical practice and biomedical research. Commercialisation of the human body, by treating it, or part of it, as a disposable economic asset is generally taken to be inconsistent with this principle. This view is not unchallenged, but insofar as it underpins current ethical thinking in Singapore, it supports a view that financial inducement to provide an organ or tissue, would amount to a form of commercialisation and is not acceptable. Furthermore, this view found strong public support during BAC's public consultation on the donation of human eggs for research. There is thus no compelling force in reason or public sentiment to depart from this view. . . .

The BAC, similarly, is interested in ensuring that neither the human body, nor any aspect of the reproductive process, becomes the subject of commercialisation. It is sensitive to the great importance attributed to the institution of the family in Singaporean society, and reproduction is a key element of this institution. Reproductive choice should remain the prerogative of the couple, and it should be free from undue influence from third parties such as researchers. For this reason, the BAC does not support the implementation of schemes whereby individuals may be financially induced to provide eggs for research. However, it considers ethically acceptable for women undergoing fertility treatment to donate eggs for research, provided that these are freely donated as gifts, without compensation, and if they are not required for future reproductive use.

Periodical and Internet Sources Bibliography

The following articles have been selected to supplement the diverse views presented in this chapter.

Asian Tribune (India)	"U.S. Cited for War Crimes: Used Terrorism Suspects as Human Guinea Pigs," June 11, 2010.
S.B. Bavdekar	"Informed Consent Documents Submitted for Initial Review: What Do They State About Compensation for Injured Research Participants?" *Indian Journal of Medical Sciences*, vol. 63, no. 10, November 2009.
Seth W. Glickman et al.	"Ethical and Scientific Implications of the Globalization of Clinical Research," *New England Journal of Medicine*, vol. 360, no. 8, February 19, 2009.
Gardiner Harris	"Concern over Foreign Trials for Drugs Sold in U.S.," *New York Times*, June 21, 2010.
Charles W. Lidz et al.	"Competing Commitments in Clinical Trials," *IRB: Ethics & Human Research*, vol. 31, no. 5, 2009
Patrick J. McDonald et al.	"Ethical Issues in Surgical Research," *Canadian Journal of Surgery*, vol. 53, no. 2, April 2010.
Joe Palca	"The Ethics of Medical Research on Children," National Public Radio, October 31, 2006. www.npr.org.
Andre Picard	"Time to End Pelvic Exams Done Without Consent," *Globe and Mail* (Canada), January 28, 2010.
Lisa Rapple	"Academic Dishonesty Is Not Just Academic," *FOCUS: Journal for Respiratory Care & Sleep Medicine*, May–June 2007.

For Further Discussion

Chapter 1

1. What are the major international articulations of medical ethics, and how are they similar? In what ways do they differ? What do you think are the most important ethical considerations a doctor should use to make important decisions regarding patient care?

2. What role might a doctor's religious convictions play in his or her ethical decision-making process? Give a few hypothetical examples where a doctor of one religious background might make a different decision than a doctor of a different religious background.

Chapter 2

1. Under what circumstances, if any, do you believe it would be ethical for a doctor to grant a patient's wish to die? What ethical rules do you think a doctor ought to follow in such a case? Use examples from the viewpoints in Chapter 2 to support your position.

2. What are the goals of palliative care? Do you think the administration of pain-killing medication is ethical when it will also shorten a terminally ill patient's life?

Chapter 3

1. After reading the viewpoints in this chapter concerning organ donation, do you believe that living donors should receive compensation for donating an organ such as a kidney? Why or why not? What kind of compensation, if any, would you find ethical?

2. According to the viewpoints in this chapter, what is the concept of "presumed consent"? How would presumed

consent address organ shortages in countries that adopt the concept as law? Do you believe that this is an ethical choice for a country to make?

Chapter 4

1. What are the ethical problems illustrated by the viewpoints in this chapter concerning the use of developing countries for clinical trials? Why do some people believe that double-blind studies in developing countries are not ethical? Should pharmaceutical companies be allowed to hold clinical trials in developing countries for drugs that are not approved for such trials in the United States or Europe?

2. What are some of the ethical problems associated with genetic research, according to the viewpoints in this chapter? In what ways do you believe it is ethical to use information derived from genetic testing?

Organizations to Contact

The editors have compiled the following list of organizations concerned with the issues debated in this book. The descriptions are derived from materials provided by the organizations. All have publications or information available for interested readers. The list was compiled on the date of publication of the present volume; the information provided here may change. Be aware that many organizations take several weeks or longer to respond to inquiries, so allow as much time as possible.

African Palliative Care Association
PO Box 72518, Kampala
  Uganda
256 414 266251 • fax: 256 414 266217
e-mail: info@apca.co.ug
website: www.apca.org.ug

The African Palliative Care Association is a nonprofit organization dedicated to providing access to, and advocating for, affordable, culturally appropriate, and high-quality palliative care for all those living in Africa. The group publishes articles, reports, and books, some of which include "Pain and Assessment Management in Sub-Saharan Africa," and "Pain Relieving Drugs in 12 African PEPFAR Countries."

American Academy of Medical Ethics (AAME)
PO Box 451, Bristol, TN   37621
(423) 844-1095
e-mail: main@ethicalhealthcare.org
website: www.ethicalhealthcare.org

The mission of the American Academy of Medical Ethics (AAME) is to advocate for the values that have underpinned Western medical care. The AAME does so by sponsoring conferences; writing articles; undertaking research; and teaching in the fields of ethics, medicine, and science. Its website includes discussions and articles on current issues such as beginning of life; cloning and stem cell research; patient care; end-of-life issues; and the medical profession.

Caring Connections

National Hospice Foundation, Washington, DC   20042-6058
(800) 658-8898
e-mail: caringinfo@nhpco.org
website: www.caringinfo.org

Caring Connections is a support and advocacy program of the National Hospice and Palliative Care Organization. It provides free resources and information to people making decisions about end-of-life care and services. Caring Connections provides on its website easy-to-read publications concerning talking about end-of-life issues, supporting someone who is grieving, caring for loved ones, talking to doctors about pain or illness, and understanding hospice and palliative care.

Center for Genetic Research Ethics and Law (CGREAL)

10900 Euclid Avenue, Cleveland, OH   44106-4976
(216) 368-2000
website: www.case.edu/med/bioethics/cgreal

The Center for Genetic Research Ethics and Law (CGREAL) studies ethical issues in human genetic research. CGREAL focuses on ethical and policy issues in the design and conduct of genetic family studies, genetic epidemiology, and genetic variation research. The organization's website includes the CGREAL newsletter, links to other medical ethics centers, news releases, and descriptions of research projects under way at the center.

Centre for Death & Society (CDAS)

Department of Social & Policy Sciences, Bath   BA2 7AY
   United Kingdom
01225 386949

e-mail: cdas@bath.ac.uk
website: www.bath.ac.uk/cdas

The Centre for Death & Society (CDAS) is the United Kingdom's only center devoted to the study and research of the social aspects of death, dying, and bereavement. Its goals are to further social, policy, and health research; provide education; enhance social policy understanding; and encourage community development. CDAS publishes the journal *Mortality*, which is available through its website.

Centre for Genetics Education (CGE)
PO Box 317, St Leonards   NSW 1590
   Australia
+61 (0) 2 9926 7324 • fax: +61 (0) 2 9906 7529
e-mail: contact@genetics.com.au
website: www.genetics.com.au

The Centre for Genetics Education (CGE) is the education arm of the New South Wales (NSW) Genetic service of NSW Health. The purpose of the center is to provide information to families and individuals as well as medical professionals. On the CGE website, students will find the CGE newsletter, *Snippets*, as well as brochures, fact sheets, pamphlets, and booklets concerning genetic testing and genetic conditions.

Coalition for Organ-Failure Solutions (COFS)
(330) 701-8399 • fax: (720) 293-0117
e-mail: cofs@cofs.org
website: www.cofs.org

The Coalition for Organ-Failure Solutions (COFS) is a nonprofit international health and human rights organization working against trafficking human organs and toward ending the exploitation of the poor as organ donors. Its activities include advocacy and support for survivors. The COFS website contains information about organ transplants and trafficking as well as the full text of the "People's Charter for Health." The site also includes videos of transplant trafficking victims telling their own stories.

Death with Dignity National Center

520 SW Sixth Avenue, Suite 1030, Portland, OR 97204
(503) 228-4415 • fax: (503) 228-7454
e-mail: info@deathwithdignity.org
website: www.deathwithdignity.org

The Death with Dignity National Center is a nonprofit advocacy organization that serves to defend the state of Oregon's Death with Dignity law. Its mission is to provide information, education, research, and support for laws that allow terminally ill patients to end their own lives. The organization's website is filled with many useful resources, including articles and links to additional resources. The "For Students" section of the website offers useful tips on researching topics related to death and dying. Students are encouraged to contact the center through the "Contact Us" link on the website.

Ethics in Medicine

Department of Bioethics and Humanities
UW Mailbox 357120
University of Washington School of Medicine
Seattle, WA 98195
fax: (206) 685-7515
e-mail: bioethx@u.washington.edu
website: http://depts.washinton.edu/bioethx

The Medical Ethics project of the University of Washington School of Medicine's Bioethics Department maintains a comprehensive database of information relating to a wide variety of ethical issues. Some of the topics covered include advanced care directives, research ethics, and physician aid in dying, among many others. Also included is a section on ethical tools that provides a clear overview of ethical principles and methodology.

Exit International

PO Box 4250, Bellingham, WA 98227
(248) 809-4435 • fax: (360) 844-1501
e-mail: contact@exitinternational.net
website: www.exitinternational.net

Exit International is an informational organization advocating for end-of-life choices that include voluntary euthanasia and assisted suicide. Exit International offers workshops, community education programs, and a support network. The organization's website offers a monthly newsletter, a blog, news releases, videos, and other information concerning end-of-life choices.

International Observatory on End of Life Care

Division of Health Research, School of Health and Medicine
Bowland Tower South, Lancaster University
Lancaster   LA1 4YT
   United Kingdom
(0)1524 593309
website: www.eolc-observatory.net

The International Observatory on End of Life Care was founded by a sociology professor at the University of Lancaster, England. Its goal is to undertake research, studies, education, and advocacy for end-of-life care for patients and caregivers. The organization offers a wide range of publications including books, reports, and journal articles, many downloadable from its website.

National Catholic Bioethics Center

6399 Drexel Road, Philadelphia, PA   19151
(215) 877-2660 • fax: (215) 877-2688
e-mail: info@ncbcenter.org
website: www.ncbcenter.org

The National Catholic Bioethics Center conducts research and education to "promote human dignity in health care . . . and derives its message directly from the teachings of the Catholic Church," according to the organization's website. The website includes frequently asked questions about bioethics as well as the full text of the Vatican's *Dignitas Personae* instruction concerning biomedical research and respect for human life. The organization also publishes a quarterly newsletter, which is available online.

National Human Genome Research Institute
National Institutes of Health, Building 31, Room 4B09
31 Center Drive, MSC 2152, 9000 Rockville Pike
Bethesda, MD   20892-2152
(301)402-9011 • fax: (301) 402-2218
website: www.genome.gov

Founded in 1997, the primary function of the National Human Genome Research Institute of the National Institutes of Health was to sequence the human genome. Now, the institute supports additional genetic research. The website offers a wide array of information, including a large section on "Issues in Genetics," which explores topics such as ethics research, genetic testing, and personalized medicine.

Bibliography of Books

Tom L. Beauchamp and James F. Childress — *Principles of Biomedical Ethics.* 6th ed. New York: Oxford University Press, 2009.

Arthur L. Caplan, James J. McCartney, and Dominic A. Sisti, eds. — *The Case of Terri Shiavo: Ethics at the End of Life.* Amherst, NY: Prometheus Books, 2006.

Annie Cheney — *Body Brokers: Inside America's Underground Trade in Human Remains.* New York: Broadway Books, 2006.

Jill A. Fisher — *Medical Research for Hire: The Political Economy of Pharmaceutical Clinical Trials.* New Brunswick, NJ: Rutgers University Press, 2009.

Kathleen Foley and Herbert Hendin, eds. — *The Case Against Assisted Suicide: For the Right to End-of-Life Care.* Baltimore, MD: Johns Hopkins University Press, 2002.

Bonnie F. Fremgen — *Medical Law and Ethics.* 3rd ed. New York: Prentice Hall, 2008.

Masha Gessen — *Blood Matters: From Inherited Illness to Designer Babies, How the World and I Found Ourselves in the Future of the Gene.* Orlando, FL: Harcourt, 2008.

Michele Goodwin — *Black Markets: The Supply and Demand of Body Parts.* New York: Cambridge University Press, 2006.

Tony Hope   *Medical Ethics: A Very Short Introduction*. New York: Oxford University Press, 2004.

Karen Judson and Carlene Harrison   *Law & Ethics for Medical Careers*. 5th ed. Boston, MA: McGraw-Hill Higher Education, 2010.

Stephen P. Kiernan   *Last Rights: Rescuing End of Life Care from the Medical System*. Waterville, ME: Thorndike Press, 2006.

Steven H. Miles   *Oath Betrayed: America's Torture Doctors*. Berkeley, CA: University of California Press, 2009.

Ronald Munson, ed.   *Intervention and Reflection: Basic Issues in Medical Ethics*. 8th ed. Belmont, CA: Thomson Wadsworth, 2008.

Michael Peel and Vincent Iaocapino, eds.   *The Medical Documentation of Torture*. New York: Cambridge University Press, 2009.

Gregory E. Pence   *Medical Ethics: Accounts of Ground-Breaking Cases*. 6th ed. New York: McGraw-Hill, 2010.

Aurora Plomer   *The Law and Ethics of Medical Research: International Bioethics and Human Rights*. London: Routledge-Cavendish, 2005.

Timothy E. Quill and Margaret P. Battin, eds.   *Physician-Assisted Dying: The Case for Palliative Care and Patient Choice*. Baltimore, MD: Johns Hopkins University Press, 2004.

Thomas A. Shannon and Nicholas J. Kockler	*An Introduction to Bioethics.* 4th ed. New York: Paulist Press, 2009.
Lesley A. Sharp	*Bodies, Commodities, and Biotechnologies: Death, Mourning, and Scientific Desire in the Realm of Human Organ Transfer.* New York: Columbia University Press, 2007.
Rebecca Skloot	*The Immortal Life of Henrietta Lacks.* New York: Crown, 2010.
Debora L. Spar	*The Baby Business: How Money, Science, and Politics Drive the Commerce of Conception.* Boston, MA: Harvard Business School Press, 2006.
Jacques P. Thiroux and Keith W. Krasemann	*Ethics: Theory and Practice.* 10th ed. New York: Prentice Hall, 2008.
Lewis Vaughan	*Bioethics: Principles, Issues and Cases.* New York: Oxford University Press, 2010.
Robert M. Veatch, Amy M. Haddad, and Dan C. English	*Case Studies in Biomedical Ethics: Decision-Making, Principles, and Cases.* New York: Oxford University Press, 2010.
David S. Wendler	*The Ethics of Pediatric Research.* New York: Oxford University Press, 2010.

Index

Geographic headings and page numbers in **boldface** refer to viewpoints about that country or region.

A

Abortion
  genetic defects, 54, 56
  organ trafficking compared, 138
  selective reduction, 54
  tissues used in vaccines, 56
  varying acceptance in ethics norms, 42
Abu Ghraib prison torture (Iraq), 17
Academic fraud, 69
Access to care and treatment
  basic rights, 26, 49, 87
  inequality in medical research and trials, 181, 182, 184–185, 186–191
  prison populations, 202, 204
  rich vs. poor nations, 182, 191
  theory vs. practice, 49–50
Access to scientific/technological developments
  basic rights, 20, 22, 26–27
  responsibility to aid poorer health infrastructures, 189–190
Acharya, Keya, 175–180
Adolescence
  communication issues of adolescents, 61–64, 66
  cultural influences, 58, 59–62, 63, 66
Advance consent, 46
Advance directives, 48, 50, 86, 89

Africa, unethical AIDS research, 181, 186–187
AIDS. *See* HIV and AIDS
Aksoy, Sahin, 48
Alder Hey scandal (United Kingdom), 140–141
Alperovitch, Annick, 49
Altruism
  egg donation, 214–215
  organ donation, 135, 139–140, 148, 149, 150–151, 157, 214–215
Alzheimer Europe, 41–50
American Medical Association (AMA)
  code of ethics, 15, 34
  human experimentation rules, 200
Amnesty International, 143
Amsterdam Forum on the Care of the Live Kidney Donor, 132
Animal experimentation, 42, 167, 182
Annas, George J., 16, 17
Antiretroviral drugs, 184–185, 186–187, 188–189, 190
Argentina, 177
Artificial insemination, 51–57
Asia
  clinical trials rates, 176, 179t
  unethical AIDS research, 181, 184–185, 186–187
  See also specific Asian countries
Assassinations, 16

Assisted suicide. *See* Physician assisted suicide/euthanasia

Australia, 58–66, 96–102
debate on medical ethics of euthanasia, 96–102
languages spoken, 65*t*
medical ethics and cultural diversity, 58–66
Australian Medical Association, 97, 101–102
Autonomy
defined, 14, 44
egg donation, 207, 209, 211–213
ethics board opinions, 46
euthanasia and, 104
medical professionals' principles, 41, 45, 46, 47–48, 82, 83, 88
organ donation value, 157
organ sales fallacy, 124, 160–161
palliative care and, 82, 83, 88
prisoner medical testing concern, 202, 204, 205
respecting, 45, 47–48, 104, 183, 207, 209
Universal Declaration on Bioethics and Human Rights, 23
AZT (AIDS drug), 184–185, 186–187, 188–189, 190

B

Barbiturates, 101
Basic health needs, 26
Belmont Report, 183
Beneficence principle, 14, 36, 46–48, 183
palliative care, 82, 88
violations, 190
Bennett, David L., 58–66
Biggins, Scott W., 145
Biocon, 177

Biodiversity protection, 22, 27
Bioethics
education, 30
European principles, 41
history of term, 42–43
medical ethics and, 81, 83
Bioethics Advisory Committee of Singapore, 206, 207–215
Blackmail of physicians, 68, 76
Bland, Anthony, 112
Blood donation, 213–214
Body/spirit connection, 142, 144
Bottle feeding, 189
Brain death, 116, 118–119, 120
Brazil, organ trade, 137, 140
Breastfeeding, 189
Bribery, 69, 72, 73, 74
British Medical Association (BMA), 34
Budiani-Saberi, Debra A., 123–134
Bunting, Madeleine, 113
Burgdorf, James R., 196

C

California
prison experimentation outlawed, 204
rules, prison executions, 15
Canada, 116–120
ethicists debate definition of death, 116–120
organ donor compensation, 153
Cancer drug trials, 177, 178–179, 195
Cancer patients
palliative care, 79, 80, 82–83, 88
right to know, 83, 85
Caplan, Arthur, 155–162
Capps, Benjamin, 212

Cardiac death, 116, 118–119

Categorical Imperative (Kant), 43

Catholic ethics

brain and cardiac death, 116, 119, 120

euthanasia and, 102

individual doctors' ethics, 36

Vatican's biomedical ethics, 51–57

Centers for Disease Control and Prevention (CDC), 177, 186–187, 189

Centre for Research on Multinational Corporations, 177

Chapple, Robin, 98

Children, as patients, 118

Chile, 16

China, 142–146, 147–154

clinical trials, 177, 179*t*

liver transplants, Queen Mary Hospital, 152*t*

organ trade reform/ eradication, 128, 142–146

organs from executed prisoners, 128, 140, 142, 143–146

volunteer organ donations cause ethical dilemmas, 147–154

Chinese medicine, 48–49

Chown, Peter, 58–66

Clinical trials

Asian rates, 176, 179*t*

ethics screening, 195

general medical ethics, 183–184, 190–191

India as destination for unethical trials, 175–180

lack of registration, 176

pharmaceutical industry pressures, and results, 182, 201–202

registration, 169

tightening of Japanese ethics guidelines, 192, 193–195, 197

unethical AIDS research and trials, 181, 184–185, 186–191

whistleblowing on unethical trials, 184–185

See also Medical research

Clinton, Bill, 186

Cloning

Human Cloning and Other Prohibited Practices Act (Singapore; 2005), 214

Vatican stance, 56

Coalition for Organ-Failure Solutions, 124, 130

Coma patients. *See* Vegetative state patients

Commodification, body products

eggs, 212, 213–215

organs and tissues, 125, 131, 137, 138–139, 157

Communication issues

adolescents, 61–64, 66

euthanasia, 92, 95, 105

family members, and palliative care, 83, 85

language differences, 60, 61, 62, 64, 65*t*, 66

nonverbal behavior, 62, 66

Compensation

egg donation, 161, 206, 208, 210, 214–215

organ donation, 153–154, 214–215

organ trafficking, 129, 130, 137, 138

prisoner medical testing, 202

surrogate motherhood, 161

See also Commodification, body products

Competence and decision-making issues

advance directives, 48, 50

capability of medical research subjects, 172

involuntary euthanasia, 111, 112–113

proxies, 50

voluntary euthanasia, 98–99, 104, 111

Conception, 52, 53

Confidentiality. *See* Privacy and confidentiality

Consent

advance consent, 46

egg donation ethics, 210–211, 214

explicit, organ donation, 157, 158

family consent, organ donations, 158–159

persons without capacity to consent, 24, 112–113, 172

"presumed consent," organ donation, 135, 140–141, 155, 159, 162

Universal Declaration on Bioethics and Human Rights, 23–24

See also Informed consent

Consequentialist ethics, 114

Corruption in medicine

Indian medical system, 67–72, 74–76, 180

medical schools, 69, 71

organ sales, 67, 68–69, 72, 74, 75

pharmaceutical field, 70, 73, 74

suggestions for eradication, 74–76

Council of Europe

Oviedo Convention on Human Rights and Biomedicine, 44, 47

Steering Committee on Bioethics, 43–44

Crimes against humanity, 15–16, 81, 170, 183, 203

Criminal physicians, India, 67–72, 74–76

Cultural diversity and pluralism, 25

Australian medical ethics, 58–66

cultural differences, 60–61, 62, 63, 64

D

Danish Council of Ethics, 46

Death, definitions and debate, 116–120

Death penalty. *See* Executions

Death with Dignity Act (Oregon, 1997), 105

Decision-making capacity. *See* Competence and decision-making issues

Declaration of Geneva, 34, 35, 81, 166

Declaration of Helsinki, 81–82, 166, 170, 178

Declaration of Istanbul on Organ Trafficking and Transplant Tourism, 131

Delmonico, Francis L., 123–134

Dementia

euthanizing patients as unacceptable, 109–112

patient fears and self-determination, 45–46

patient treatment and vulnerability, 50

Deontology of medical ethics, 41–42, 81

Dignitas Personae, 51–57

Dignity. *See* Human dignity

Distributive justice, 49, 50, 156, 183, 190

Diversity. *See* Cultural diversity and pluralism

"Do no harm" principle. *See* Non-maleficence principle

Do not resuscitate (DNR) policies, 86

Doctor-patient relations
corrupt doctors, 68, 69, 70, 72
medical research separateness, 174
moral codes and understandings, 37, 39, 40
more to less paternalistic, 48
trust, and legalized euthanasia, 105, 113
trust, and organ donations, 162

Donor cards, 139–140, 158, 159, 162

Donum Vitae, 52, 55

Doyal, Len, 90–95

Drug companies. *See* Pharmaceutical companies

Drug toxicity studies, 201

Drug trials. *See* Clinical trials

Duin, Julia, 51–57

E

Egg donation
markets/egg scarcity, 161, 212
research purposes, 206, 207–215

Egypt, organ trade, 127, 129–130

Eli Lilly, 201

Embryos
adoption, 51–52, 57
egg donation and embryo creation, 210
personhood status, 52, 53–54, 56

End-of-life processes, and palliative care, 86, 88–89

Englaro, Eluana, 118

Environmental protection, 27

Epistemological authority, 37

Equality of care, 49–50, 83

Equality principles, 25, 41, 43, 49–50, 208

Ethical codes. *See* Philosophical ethical codes; Professional ethical codes; Religious ethical codes

Ethics committees and review boards
clinical trials, 179, 180, 182, 185
Japan, guidelines and improvements, 192, 193, 194–195, 197
purposes, 29

Eugenics
genetic manipulation and engineering, 57
preimplantation genetic diagnosis, 54, 56

Europe/European Union, 41–50, 155–162
EU formation, 43–44
EU opposes sale of human organs, 155–162
medical professionals guided by ethical principles, 41–50
research ethics surveillance, 197
unethical clinical trials, 178

Euthanasia
debate banned, Ireland, 90–95
debate of ethics, Australia, 96–102
definitions and terminology, 87, 94, 97
legal, certain countries, 87, 101
palliative care as better alternative, 87
patient desires, 87, 94
public support, Australia, 97–98

should be illegal in the UK, 109–115

should be legal in the UK, 103–108

system reform proposals, 91–95

varying acceptance in ethics norms, 42

Vatican stance, 56

Executions

organs from executed prisoners, 128, 140, 142, 143–146

prison doctors actions/ethics, 14–15

F

Family relations

adolescents, and cultural considerations, 59, 62, 63–64

aggressive care opinions, 83, 86

assisted suicide, 106t

caregivers, and dementia, 109, 110–111

caregivers, and euthanasia, 98–99, 109, 110–111

life support decisions, 118

organ donations, 126, 136, 147, 153, 154, 158–159, 162

palliative care, 83, 85, 86

Faunce, T.A., 28

FDA (U.S. Food and Drug Administration), 201

Fertility technologies. See Reproductive technologies

Finnish National Advisory Board on Health Care Ethics, 46

Florida, prison executions, 15

Free choice. See Autonomy

Freezing of embryos, 51, 52, 53–54

Future generations, consideration, 27, 208

G

Gender considerations, 63

Gender testing, prenatal, 70

Gene therapies, 57

Genetic defects

gene therapy, 57

preimplantation diagnosis, 54, 56

Genetic engineering

egg donation, 210

induced pluripotent stem cells and, 177–178

Vatican stance, 57

Genetic makeup

preimplantation diagnosis, 54, 56

protecting future generations, 27, 208

Genetic reproductive technologies, Vatican opinions, 51–57

Gift relationship

egg donation, 214–215

organ donation, 135, 139–140, 148, 149, 150–151, 157, 214–215

Gillon, Raanan, 50

"Good death," 83, 86

Guantánamo Bay detention facility, 17

H

Harris, John, 106

Harvard University, 184, 188

Hassani, Behzad, 181–191

Heart transplants, 119–120

See also Organ donation and transplants

Hellegers, André, 43

Hippocrates, 81

Hippocratic Oath, 34, 35, 36–37, 38, 81

See also Non-maleficence principle

HIV and AIDS

pain, 85

unethical research trials, 181, 184–185, 186–191

HIV services, 84

Home end-of-life care, 86

Honesty. *See* Truthfulness values

Hong Kong

liver transplants, Queen Mary Hospital, 152*t*

volunteer organ donations cause ethical dilemmas, 147–154

Hood, Dennis, 99–100

Hospitals

Catholic, procedures, 119

ethics committees, 194, 195, 213

vs. home care, 86

Indian corruption, 68, 69, 70–71

organ donation policies, 138–139, 149, 153, 158–159

Hoy, David Couzens, 42

Human Cloning and Other Prohibited Practices Act (Singapore; 2005), 214

Human dignity

Catholic values, 56

medical and biomedical principles, 21, 22, 25, 32, 41, 43, 44, 82

organ donation principles, 157

religious principles, 37, 56

Human experimentation and research

legal representation, 23

Nazi physicians, 15–16, 81, 170, 183, 203

prisoners, 198–205

Tuskegee experiments (1932-1972), 185–186, 198, 200

World Medical Association, ethical principles, 165–174

See also Clinical trials

Human rights

human objectification and commodification, 125, 131, 137, 138–139, 157, 161

Oviedo Convention on Human Rights and Biomedicine (Council of Europe), 44, 47

palliative care, 84, 87, 88

prisoners, in organ trade, 142, 144

prisoners, medical testing, 198, 202, 203, 204

professional ethics decisions, 37, 39

Universal Declaration on Bioethics and Human Rights, 20–32, 40

Human Rights Watch, reports, 84

Human vulnerability, 24

I

Immigrant populations, 59, 60, 62, 66

In vitro fertilization

egg donation, 211

Vatican stance, 53, 57

India, 67–76, 79–89, 175–180

government corruption, 69

government's failures in public health, 67, 70–71

legislation and regulation, 175, 179

medical ethics foundations, 79, 81–82

medical profession, corruption and abuse, 67–76

organ trade, 67, 68–69, 72, 74, 127, 130, 140, 145

palliative care following ethical guidelines, 79–89
unethical clinical trials, 175–180
Indian Council of Medical Research (ICMR), 178–179, 180
Indian Medical Association, 71
Induced pluripotent stem cells (ips cells), 177–178
Infant mortality rates, 191
Infanticide
   active euthanasia, 114
   dangers, 56
Information sharing. *See* Informed consent; Truthfulness values
Informed consent, 23
   egg donation, 206, 207, 208, 209, 210–211, 213
   family member duties, 83
   medical research subjects, 23, 165, 167, 170–172, 183, 194, 195
   organ donation, 158
   terminal patients, 83, 87
   uninformed patients, and physicians' rights, 45
Innovations. *See* Medical discoveries and technologies
Institute of Medicine (IOM), 199, 201–202, 205
International guidelines
   bioethics, 20–32, 166
   medical research, 165–174, 183
Interpreters, 64
Interrogation methods, 17
Iran
   organ trafficking, 130
   regulated organ market, 160
Iraq War, 2003-, 17
Ireland, 90–95
Irish Council for Bioethics, 94
Islamic medical ethics, 48

J

Japan, 192–197
Japanese Ministry of Health, Labour and Welfare, 192, 193–195
Jewish ethics, 36
Johns Hopkins University and Hospital, 177, 178–179
Johnson & Johnson, 177, 182
Johnstone, Anne, 135–141
Journal of the American Medical Association (JAMA), 200–201
Justice principles, 49–50, 82, 87, 88, 208
   See also Access to care and treatment; Access to scientific/technological developments; Distributive justice

K

Kang, Melissa S.-L., 58–66
Kant, Immanuel, 43, 44
Kantian ethics, 36–37, 39, 43, 44
Kao, Grace, 48–49
Kelly, Eugene, 50
Kidney donations and sales. *See* Organ donation and transplants; Organ trade
Kuwait Statement (national organ donation practices), 131–132

L

Laidlaw, Stuart, 116–120
Language differences and difficulties, 60, 61, 62, 64, 65*t*, 66
Lee, Ella, 147–154
Lethal injections, 14–15
Letrozole (medication), 177
Levada, William J., 51–52
Life expectancy, 135, 136, 138

Life-saving measures, and pallia-tive care, 86, 88–89
Liver transplants, 147, 148–150
See also Organ donation and transplants
Löfmark, Rurik, 99*t*

M

Maastricht Treaty (1992), 43
Mahajan, Vijay, 67–76
Malaria research, 177, 200
Masuda, Koji, 192–197
Mawlana, 48
Medical Council of India, 71, 74
Medical discoveries and technolo-gies
  access rights, 20, 22, 26–27
  knowledge sharing, 22, 31
Medical education corruption, 69, 71
Medical ethics principles. *See* Au-tonomy; Beneficence principle; Distributive justice; Justice prin-ciples; Non-maleficence principle
Medical ethics system, 28, 41–42, 183–184
Medical experimentation. *See* Hu-man experimentation and re-search
Medical histories
  adolescents, 62, 63
  psychosocial history, 62
Medical literature, 173, 200–201
Medical negligence, 71–72
Medical research
  animal subjects, 42, 167, 182
  combined with medical care, 174
  Declaration of Helsinki, 81–82, 166, 170, 178
  eggs, donated for research, 206–215

freedom and rights, 20, 21
informed consent, 23, 165, 167, 170–172, 183, 194, 195, 206, 207, 210–211
Japan, national status, 196
Japanese ethical guidelines, 192–197
population representation, 166, 169, 172
publishing results, 173, 200–201
research protocols, 168–169, 209–210
studies by region, *188*
transnational practices, 29–30
unethical clinical trials and research, 175–180, 181–191
World Medical Association principles, 165–174
Mental competency. *See* Compe-tence and decision-making issues
Merion, Robert M., 128
Miles, Steven H., 38
Military physicians, 14
Mill, John Stuart, 45
Mohan, Harit, 179
Mohanti, Bidhu K., 79–89
Montalva, Eduardo Frei, 16
Morphine, 84, 85, 86, 114
Mukherjee, Debarati, 142–146
Multiculturalism. *See* Cultural di-versity and pluralism

N

National Academy of Sciences, Institute of Medicine, 199, 201–202, 205
National AIDS Research Institute (NARI) (India), 180
National health expenditures, 70
National Institutes of Health (NIH), 83, 184, 186–187, 188, 189

Nazi-era Germany human experimentation, 15–16, 81, 170, 183, 203
Negligence cases, 71–72
Nepal, 177
Netherlands euthanasia laws and rates, 103, 105, 106–107
New York Times (newspaper), 186, 200, 204
Nigeria, 177
Nightingale Pledge, 81
Nitschke, Philip, 100, 101
Non-discrimination principles, 25
Non-maleficence principle
  dictatorships' power and control, 15–16
  doctors' participation in torture, 16, 17
  medical ethics base, 14, 45, 46–48, 81, 82, 83, 161, 183, 190
  palliative care, 82, 83, 88
Non-voluntary euthanasia, 92, 94–95
  babies, 114
  dangers of increases where euthanasia is legal, 106
  declining rates where euthanasia is legal, 103, 105, 106–107
Nonverbal behavior, 62, 66
North Carolina, prison executions, 15
Novartis, 177
Novo Nordisk, 177
Nuremberg Principles/Code, 16, 81, 170, 183, 205
Nuremberg Trials (1946), 16
Nursing ethics, 81

O

Opioids, 85–86
"Opt-out" systems. *See* Presumed consent in organ donation

Oregon euthanasia laws and rates, 103, 105, 106, 107
Organ donation and transplants
  challenges, India, 72, 74, 75, 76
  Chinese programs, 142, 143
  donor cards, 139–140, 158, 159, 162
  donor compensation, 153–154, 214–215
  European ethical framework, 155, 156–159
  Hong Kong ethical dilemmas, 147–154
  legal transplant tourism, 126
  presumed consent, 135, 140–141, 155, 159, 162
  risks, 147, 149, 150, 151, 161
  selflessness principles, 135, 139–140, 148, 149, 150–151, 157
  timing and methods, 116, 117, 118–120
  transplant programs, 75, 131–132
  UK statistics, 139
  waiting list patients, 139, 141, 156
Organ trade, 75
  Chinese trade and reform attempts, 128, 140, 142, 143–146
  considered unethical worldwide, 123–134
  definitions, 125–126, 131
  ethical protocols needed, 130–133
  European Union opposition, 155–162
  follow-up care needs, donors, 124, 130, 138, 145–146
  follow-up care needs, recipients, 128–129
  India, 67, 68–69, 72, 74, 127, 140, 145

market economies, 131, 136–138, 159–160

markets, regulated, 160, 162

markets, studies, 123, 124, 126–130

U.S. recipients, 128–129, 140

Organ "transplant tourism," 125–129, 138

   China, 142, 145, 146

   protocols and reform, 130–131

Otsuka, 177

Overtreatment, 70, 82–83, 86

Oviedo Convention on Human Rights and Biomedicine, 44, 47

P

Pain, 85

Pakistan

   clinical trials, 179*t*

   organ trade, 123, 126, 129, 130, 145

Palliative care

   following ethical guidelines, India, 79–89

   limitations of pain relief, 103, 105

   option, vs. aggressive cancer treatments, 82–83

   research ethics challenges, 87–88

Parent-child relations, 63–64

Parnell, Mark, 98–99, 102

Patient autonomy. *See* Autonomy

Patient competence. *See* Competence and decision-making issues

Patient confidentiality. *See* Privacy and confidentiality

Patient consent. *See* Consent; Informed consent

Patient-doctor relations. *See* Doctor-patient relations

Patients' rights

   laws as source for medical ethics, 42

   medical research, and patient awareness, 195

   right to know, 83–84, 85

   right to medical care, 26, 49, 87

Penicillin, 185–186

Personhood of embryos, 52, 53–54, 56

Peru, 177

Pfizer, 177

Pharmaceutical companies

   involvement in organ trade, 133

   market pressures, and results, 182, 201–202

   prisoner medical testing, U.S., 198, 199, 200–202, 204–205

   unethical clinical trials and research, 175, 176–180, 181–191

Pharmacists, corruption, 70, 73, 74

Philippines, organ trade, 123, 126–127, 128, 130, 145

Phillips, Melanie, 109–114

Philosophical ethical codes

   autonomy, 39, 43, 44–46, 47–48

   precedence over professional codes, 33, 36–37, 39, 40

Physician assisted suicide/euthanasia

   community polls, 106*t*

   con- stance, 109–115

   defined, 94

   doctor polls, 99*t*

   pro- stance, 103, 104–108

   See also Euthanasia; Voluntary euthanasia

Physicians' rights to refuse consent, 36, 45

Pin, Lim, 206–215
Pinochet, Augusto, 16
Placebo, in medical studies, 173, 181, 187–189, 190, 191
Poor
  medical testing populations, 201
  organ trade exploitation, 68–69, 123, 124, 129, 130, 134, 135, 137–138, 140, 160–161
  patient exploitation, India, 68–69, 70–71, 72, 74, 140
Potter, Van Rensselaer, 42–43
Prayer of Maimonides, 35
Preimplantation genetic diagnosis, 54, 56
Prenatal care, 189, 191
Presumed consent in organ donation
  countries with active policies, 159, 162
  European policy arguments, 155, 159
  Scotland, 135, 140–141
"Primum non nocere". See Non-maleficence principle
Prison abuse, 200, 202, 203, 204
Prisoners
  health characteristics, 203
  medical testing, United States, 198–205
  medical testing ethics, debate history, 200–201, 203
  organ trade, China, 128, 140, 142, 143–146
Privacy and confidentiality
  breaches allowed, professional ethics codes, 34–35
  doctor-family communications, 83
  egg donation, 207, 209, 210
  ethics guidelines principle, 25, 207

medical research subjects, 167, 171
Professional ethical codes
  sources, 34, 39–40, 42
  variance and conflicts, 33–40
Proportionality principles, 46–47, 165, 206, 208
Publishing, medical research, 173, 200–201
Purdy, Debbie, 104, 108

Q

Queen Mary Hospital, Hong Kong, 152t
Quinlan, Karen Ann, 118

R

Rationality, 44
Reciprocity principles, 207–208
Regulatory bodies, national, 175, 179, 182
Reincarnation beliefs, 142
Religious ethical codes
  euthanasia opinions, 102
  organ donation decisions and, 142, 144, 150
  precedence over professional codes, 33, 36, 37, 40
  See also Catholic ethics; Islamic medical ethics
Reproductive technologies
  Catholic ethics, 51–57
  commercialization avoidance, 215
  egg donation, 210, 211, 212, 213
Research, medical. See Clinical trials; Medical research; Research protocols
Research protocols, 168–169, 209–210

Right to die

vs. duty to die, 112–113

patients' rights, euthanasia, 97, 100, 103, 104

See also Euthanasia; Physician assisted suicide/euthanasia; Voluntary euthanasia

Right to refuse consent (physicians), 36, 45

Right to refuse treatment

patients' right to die, 97, 100, 102

patients' rights and self-determination/autonomy, 45, 46

Risks, patient/subject

egg donation, 206, 209–210, 213

inherent in clinical trials, 194

medical research informing, 165, 167, 169, 171

organ donation, 147, 149, 150, 151, 161

Rosner, Fred, 14

Rossiter, Christian, 97, 98, 100, 102

Royal College of Obstetricians and Gynaecologists (UK), 114

Royal College of Physicians (United Kingdom), 104

Rumsfeld, Donald, 17

Russia, 177

S

Schiavo, Terri, 118

Scotland, 135–141

organ donation snapshot, 139

presumed consent for organ donation would solve shortage, 135–141

Selective reduction, 54

Self-determination, 45–46

See also Autonomy

Sex determination tests, 70

Sexual assault of patients, 68

Shantha Biotechnics, 177

Shimazono, Yosuke, 127–128

Sikora, Joanna, 102

Singapore, 206–215

clinical trials, 179*t*

ethics of donating eggs for research, 206–215

organ donor compensation, 153

presumed consent, organ donation, 162

Slavery, 155, 157

"Slippery slope" arguments

biotechnology dangers, 44

voluntary euthanasia may lead to involuntary euthanasia, 112–113

voluntary euthanasia will not lead to involuntary euthanasia, 95, 103, 106–107

Slovenia, organ trade, 123, 127

Social and health responsibilities, 26

Solvay Pharmaceuticals, 177

Southern Hemisphere

Declaration of Helsinki input and review, 178

unethical AIDS research practices, 181–191

State medical boards, and prison executions, 15

Stem cell research

egg donation, 210, 212

unethical/illegal clinical trials, 175, 177–178

Stem cells
  induced pluripotent (iPS cells), 177–178
  sources' relevance, for Vatican, 56
  therapeutic uses, 56
Stereotyping, 62
Stone, T. Howard, 203
Such, Bob, 98
Suicide, 98, 108
  See also Physician assisted suicide/euthanasia
Sun Pharmaceutical, 177
Surrogate motherhood
  markets, 161
  Vatican stance, 51, 53
Surveillance, ethics guidelines, 192, 193, 194, 197
Sustainability principles, 27, 208
Swiss Academy of Medical Sciences, 49
Syphilis research, 185–186, 198, 200

T

Tallis, Raymond, 103–108
Tenik, Ali, 48
Terminal diagnoses
  considering dying patients "dead," 118
  euthanasia laws, 98, 103, 104
  patient information sharing, 37, 39, 83, 85
Terminally ill patients' care. *See* Palliative care
Thailand, unethical AIDS research, 181, 184–185, 186
Therapeutic cloning, 56
Time of death, 116

Torture
  illness suffering as, and government responsibilities, 84
  state regimes, 15–16
  wartime issues, 17
Tourism, organ transplants. *See* Organ "transplant tourism"
Toxicity studies, 201
Trafficking of organs. *See* Organ trade
Trafficking of persons, 155, 157
Transnational ethics practices, 29–30
Transplantation of Human Organs Act (1994), 72
The Transplantation Society, 124, 133
Treaty on European Union (1992), 43
Truthfulness values
  medical ethics component, 79, 82, 83, 88
  professional and personal ethics, 36–37, 39
  See also Patients' rights
Tuberculosis, 124, 145–146
Tuskegee experiments (1932-1972), 185–186, 198, 200

U

Uganda, 177
Unethical practices. *See* Corruption in medicine
United Kingdom, 103–108, 109–115
  euthanasia should be illegal, 109–115
  euthanasia should be legal, 103–108, 106t
  organ donation snapshot, 139

organ donor compensation, 153

presumed consent, organ donation, 135, 140–141

United Nations Educational, Scientific and Cultural Organization (UNESCO), Universal Declaration on Bioethics and Human Rights, 20–32, 40

United Nations Office on Drugs and Crime, 125

United Network for Organ Sharing (UNOS), 125–126

United States, 198–205

American recipients of organ trade, 128–129, 140

organ donor compensation, 153

prisoner medical testing, 198–205

Tuskegee experiments (1932-1972), 185–186, 198, 200

University research

Harvard University, 184, 188

Japan, 196

Johns Hopkins University, 177, 178–179

prisoner medical testing, 204–205

U.S. Army, 184–185

U.S. Food and Drug Administration (FDA), 201

U.S. National Institutes of Health, 177

Utilitarian ethics, 36–37

V

Vaccine production, 56

Vatican, 51–57

Veatch, Robert M., 33–40

Vegetative state patients

death definitions, 117, 118

euthanasia and withdrawal of care, 112–113

Vergara, Benjamin, 16

Vioxx (drug), 201

Vitelli, Kaylee, 118, 119, 120

Voluntary euthanasia

debated, 87, 96, 97–102

defined, 94

Voluntary organ donation. *See* Organ donation and transplants

W

Waiting lists, organ transplants, 139, 141, 156, 160

Walter Reed Army Institute of Research, 177

War, effects on medical values/ethics, 14

See also World War II, Nazi medical practices

War on Terror, 17

Warnock, Geoffrey, 114

Warnock, Mary, 109–112, 113–114, 115

Washington Post (newspaper), 184–185

Waterboarding, 17

Wemos Foundation, 176, 177, 178

Wiegand, Timothy J., 198–205

Williams, John R., 170

Withholding of diagnoses, 37, 39

Withholding of treatment

instead of euthanasia, 92–94, 99*t*, 107, 108, 112–113

terminal cancer patients, 83

World Health Organization (WHO)

corruption and pharmaceuticals, 73

organ trade research and reports, 124, 126–128, 131–133, 134, 138, 144, 145
palliative care work, 85
World Medical Association (WMA)
Declaration of Geneva, 34, 35, 81, 166
Declaration of Helsinki, 81–82, 166, 170, 178

International Code of Medical Ethics, 166
medical research ethical principles, 165–174
World War II, Nazi medical practices, 15–16, 81, 170, 183, 203

Z

Zukerman, Wendy, 96–102